CONTEMPORARY
ISSUES FOR
EVANGELICAL
CHRISTIANS

CONTEMPORARY ISSUES FOR EVANGELICAL CHRISTIANS

DAVID L. McKENNA

CONTEMPORARY DISCUSSION SERIES

BAKER BOOK HOUSE
Grand Rapids, Michigan

PHOTOLITHOPRINTED BY CUSHING - MALLOY, INC.
ANN ARBOR, MICHIGAN, UNITED STATES OF AMERICA
1979

In **Contemporary Issues for Evangelical Christians** Dave McKenna has provided fresh insights in a readable, thought-provoking style. It is a personal book by a personable and gifted evangelical leader — a book which blends commentary with the punch and wisdom of biblical truth.

Dr. McKenna writes with the authority of one who has grappled with the issues. On gambling, he speaks from experience as chairman of a special state control commission. When he bares conflicting thoughts on euthanasia, he writes out of the anguishing time surrounding his father's death. In examining the abortion dilemma, he probes the legal, medical, moral, and spiritual aspects of the question.

This book touches us all right where we live, and addresses contemporary concerns which trouble evangelicals everywhere.

Billy A. Melvin
Executive Director
National Association of Evangelicals

CONTENTS

Preface 9

1. Who Put the Alarm Clock in My Ivory Tower? 11

2. Are You Willing to Bet on Legalized Gambling? 19

3. O Medical Death, Where Is Thy Sting? 31

4. If "R" Is Rotten, What Is "PG"? 41

5. How About the Victims in No-Fault Divorce? .. 47

6. Do the Unborn Need a Bill of Rights? 53

7. Is Punishment by Death a Capital Idea? 65

8. Why Aren't Christians in Jail
   Where They Belong? 73

9. How Do You Tell a Poor Man
   that God Loves Him? 79

10. Is This the Women's ERA? 89

11. What Do You Do When the Pump Runs Dry? ... 99

12. Why Do We Make Play Such Hard Work? 105

13. Have you Heard the Prophecy
    According to *Sports Illustrated*? 111

14. Has Even Satanism Gone to the Devil? 117

15. Are the Signs of the Times
    Written in the Wind? 123

16. Will the Last Person to Leave
    Please Turn Out the Light? 129

17. Do I Have to Stay Awake, Lord? 137

PREFACE

In a classic *Peanuts* cartoon, Linus insists that a baby brother begin to walk. Lucy, watching the struggle with a cynical eye, scolds, "Don't rush him. After all, once you begin to walk, you are committed for life."

Before the eyes of the world, evangelical Christians have begun to walk. Visible, straight up and in motion, we are committed for life. No longer can we claim smallness or weakness to avoid responsibility. Straight on, we are being asked, "What difference will the new birth make in an old world?"

Unlike Lucy, the question is one of need, not cynicism. A quiet desperation pervades our individual and collective spirits. Social freedom is ours, but only at the price of moral meaning. Scientific progress is ours, but only at the price of ethical confusion. Somehow, some way, the evidence of spiritual rebirth and the need for moral renewal must find each other.

Awakened, informed and active Christians are the answer. Beginning with the redemptive experience which energizes new creations in Christ Jesus, born-again believers must stand up before the world with personal wholeness and moral integrity. Then the walk begins. One step will lead to a tenderizing of spirit and another to a quickening of mind until human hurts and moral conflicts are unavoidable issues. There, the path divides. Some deny responsibility, others shift the blame, still others send money, but a few assume the responsibility to understand in order to act. For a Christian, understanding means reading, listening and talking about moral issues, but not in the hollow chamber of an ethical vacuum. The search turns around the Word of God for revealed promises and upon the Holy Spirit for guidance in the gaps. Sooner or later, then, the walker must stop and say, "Here I stand, so help me God." Not that the knowledge is complete or that the walk has ended, but with the firmness of the conviction that time leaves no alternative. Once this far, there is no turning back. Action dictates giant strides into some arena of moral conflict where the danger can be covered only by the promise that "We have this treasure in earthen vessels. . . " (II Cor. 4:7)

Contemporary Issues for Evangelical Christians is the journal of an awakened conscience. Each chapter is the log of a struggle just begun. Now I invite you to join me. Questions at the end of each chapter will let you advance your reading and discussion at the point where I left off. More than that, I invite you to join me in the arena where the issues are drawn and in doubt. *You* may be the certain sound of truth for which the world awaits.

— David L. McKenna

1

Who Put the Alarm Clock
in My Ivory Tower?

During the French Revolution, Robespierre said, "Give me thirty words from the pen of any man and I'll hang him." His overstatement points up a sober truth. Writing, as well as preaching, is a dangerous business. James might have added the pen to the tongue when he wrote, "How great a matter a little fire kindleth" (James 3:5). I know what he means, because I have lived to witness my own spiritual hanging by the words I have written.

Like a one-string banjo player, I have dedicated my "In the World" column in *Action* magazine to the proposition that evangelical Christians must risk their witness in the moral morass of contemporary life. Past columns have dealt with such issues as abortion, pornography, economic equality, ecology, divorce, euthanasia, prison riots, racism, and sexism. Sentences such as these will sound familiar to those who have followed the column or heard me say:

The ethical revolution toward a no-fault society may be an alarm clock for a sleeping church.

We may try to influence public policy and practice by calling the world to accountability before God.

Biblical social concern is not an option for a Christian.

Sincerity is not a question as I recall these words. They were written with honesty and conviction, but like so many sermons and scholarly dissertations, they had never been judged by the twin tests of reality and risk. Reality cannot be tested from an ivory tower any more than risk can be tested from behind the pulpit.

Then it happened! In the middle of the Christmas holidays, when the campus was quiet, the radio was tuned to Christmas carols, and the greeting cards read "Peace on Earth," a telephone call came from the governor's office. An authoritative voice at the other end of the line said, "The governor wants you to chair his statewide *Ad Hoc* Committee on Gambling."

Never again will I be hard on the man who begged for time to kiss his bride good-bye, wrap up his business, or take care of his family before he followed Jesus. Why would the governor ask a nongambling man of the cloth and a politically naive educator to take such an assignment? The answer came back, "The people have voted to liberalize gambling, but caution is needed; and we are all concerned about the quality of life in our state. We want a man with good credentials, in whom the public has confidence." Flattery aside, if the governor is concerned about the quality of life in his state, how can a citizen and a Christian avoid his responsibility?

Still, the first impulse was to say no, but, like Macbeth's "Amen," the no stuck in my throat. Then, I thought about asking for a safer assignment. Finally, I begged for time. A ten-day reprieve was granted, and I began a troubled process of reasoning, prayer, and consultation. In the end, however, it was a lonely decision which can be traced through several turning points.

Reason dictated a negative decision. Time-demands in college and community affairs had already reached the breaking point. I was like the man who was honored for being a 100 percenter. His response was, "I didn't intend it that way, but I kept giving pieces of my time away until there were no pieces left." Something had to give and, as usual, the first line of sacrifice would be my family, because college demands would never go away.

Strangely enough, ego also voted no. It was doubtful that anyone would actively seek the Chairmanship of the Gambling Committee as a political plum. In fact, I desperately wanted to know how many others had already turned it down. Politicians, they say, would rather be stoned than ignored; but I would rather be liked than visible. The hot seat at the head of the Gambling Committee was not the kind of attention I wanted or needed.

All of the arguments that I marshaled against accepting the appointment came into focus in my role as a college president and minister representing an evangelical Christian constituency. The people of the state had overwhelmingly voted for the liberalization of gambling laws. The governor himself had said that he would not oppose a statewide lottery. Therefore, if I accepted the assignment, I had everything to lose and nothing to gain. As a nongambling minister at the head of a college with a nongambling rule, my constituents would undoubtedly expect me to reverse the vote to liberalize gambling. That bridge had already been crossed. The governor wanted caution, but the will of the people dictated change. Sooner or later, I would have to report for the Committee in favor of certain types of gambling. Imagine the misunderstanding that would arise among evangelical Christians who heard that legalized gambling was introduced into the state of Washington by the "McKenna Committee." At the other extreme would be the wealthy and powerful gambling lobby. Unless the Committee recommended wide opening of Las Vegas-type games, the gambling interests would call "foul," because a minister headed the

Committee. In psychology, that's called an "avoidance-avoidance" situation from which both fools and angels run.

Rationally, there was no alternative to a negative answer. The heart has ways, however, that the head cannot know. Intuition was still leading me to say yes. I recalled the boldness of my words about an "evangelical avant-garde" and "ministers without portfolio" who are exposed on all fronts at once. Having chided evangelical Christians for making ethical pronouncements when it was either safe or too late, it was not time to test the witness where the issue was still in doubt. Slowly, but surely, I had been weaving a cord of words that now became a noose around my neck. Wasn't it Frank Laubach who said, "When I stand before God, He will not ask to see my trophies, but my scars"?

God's recent leading of my life also began to make sense. In devotional readings, two new insights had come to me. One was to discover a new dimension of Christian witness when Jesus said, "Ye are the salt of the earth" (Matthew 5:13). All of my life I had talked about the "redemptive influence" of Christians. Salt, however, is not a redemptive agent; it is a preservative. Christians have a responsibility for preserving the world as well as redeeming it. While the Chairmanship of the Gambling Committee would not be considered a redemptive witness, it could be a preservative witness. I knew then what God was trying to teach me.

Equal force for a positive response came from Paul's description of his own calling in Romans 15. My wife and I were reading the chapter together one morning when I discovered the revolutionary character of Paul's ministry. He said that he did not preach anything which God had not already worked in him. He also said that he would not preach where other men had preached. If these two motives were put into practice by Christians today, evangelical gimmicks would not be needed. Rather than worrying about others, however, I had to ask myself whether or not my sense of ministry was as well defined as was Paul's. I concluded that God had called me to minister to the power of the gospel through Christian higher education to a secular world. Perhaps the governor's request was the secular phase of that ministry.

The invitation was also a test of my leadership at Seattle Pacific University. Several years ago, a decision was made to move to Seattle and become part of a Christian liberal arts college in the center of the city. I had the strong conviction that the future of evangelical Christianity would turn upon an urban pivot. Early in my administration, I had called for a curriculum in which the city, with its riches and its rubble, would become our campus. Later, the faculty approved a new curriculum which included a five-hour internship in the city for our students. After considerable debate, the term "crucible" was adopted to describe the experience, because it meant a test for learning and faith in the rough-and-tumble of the real world. As the potential for the "crucible" began to open up, the thought came to me that the experience ought to become a part of a faculty member's development, as well as a student's. Armed with this radical thought, I planned to present the challenge to the faculty at the first opportunity. Then, alas, the governor's call came, and it meant that the college president had to enter the "crucible" first.

The final straw for the camel's sagging back came from a strange source. On the day the decision had to be made, Victor Reisel, the acid-blinded columnist, reported that organized crime was buying low-cost land throughout the nation. With the wisdom of serpents, he said that the syndicate was anticipating Las Vegas-type gambling in every state in the union in the near future. Having weighed my convictions as a Christian and as an educator, the decision to say yes came when I accepted my share of responsibility as a citizen for the quality of life in our state.

Later that day, I said yes, but not without misgivings. It was like walking out of the Garden of Eden and looking back as the angels crossed flaming swords to block my return forever. Then, the fear came. I was all alone and had self-doubts about my ability to survive in the political jungle. Yet, the sense of "ought" was so great that any other alternative would have been defeat. Without the drama of Luther's "Here I stand" or the import of Christ's words, "Not my will, but thine, be done" (Luke 22:42), I simply passed through the point of no return, knowing that the decision was right. Since that time, I have had the opportunity to find out what it means to be involved. The criticism which I anticipated has not yet come. Most people have said that they trust my decision, even though it came as a surprise. Having steeled myself for antagonism, I did not anticipate the barbs of good humor. One "Letter to the Editor" compared the governor's appointment of a minister to Chair the Gambling Committee to the pope asking the devil to guard the holy font. In another instance, an alumnus called to tell about the time that he was caught by the president in a dice game in a dormitory and marched off to the office for prayer and reprimand. He laughed. "How times have changed."

In the Committee itself, the conflict of vested interests in the gambling question surfaced early. As chairman, I had not only the practical problem of balancing those interests but also that of discreetly entering into the debate at critical moments with the nonecclesiastical words of a "preservative" witness. Because politics is the "practical art of the possible," it was soon obvious that the Committee would take a position in favor of gambling. This, as chairman, I would have to report to the public, but with the privilege of either participation in a minority report or a personal statement.

"Crucible" is no longer an academic word to me. Literally, it means "a vessel of clay in which precious metals are refined under intense heat." So far, I have learned the meaning of a "vessel of clay" and "intense heat." Whether results as valuable as "precious metals" are achieved remains to be seen. Prior to each meeting, however, the power of the promise of II Corinthians 4:7 has given me strength and confidence: "But we have this treasure in earthen vessels, that the excellency of the power may be of God, and not of us."

QUESTIONS

1. Jesus said, "Ye are the salt of the earth . . ." (Matt. 5:13). Since salt is a preservative agent which savors the world and keeps it from rotting, what are some of the specific centers of contemporary life in which Christians should lead and act in order to savor and preserve the quality of life in a secular society?

2. Some churches have commissioning services for lay persons who are moving into new areas of secular responsibility. Who are some of the people in your church who might be commissioned as your "ministers without portfolio" in their profession and public witness?

3. A secular society is unredeemed and we cannot expect its people

to live as Christians. Should we then impose our standards of morality upon other people by legal or legislative action? Does the Bible give us a principle or does Christ give us an example of how we should approach the world?

4. If you were to apply to your own life Paul's principles to preach only what he had experienced and only where others had not preached (Rom. 15:18-20), what witness could you, and you alone, take to a special group of unreached people?

5. Assume that you have just been called to serve on the human rights commission for your community. On the commission agenda will be complaints of discrimination from racial minorities, women, homosexuals, the elderly, and the handicapped. In weighing your decision as a citizen and a Christian, what risks would you have to take as a member of the commission? What are some of the unique opportunities for Christian witness that membership might provide? Do you feel as if you would accept or reject the appointment? Why?

2

Are You Willing to Bet
on Legalized Gambling?

At a business lunch one day, an attorney explained why he openly opposed his father who headed the state racing commission. One fact had convinced him. Daily bets at the horse track averaged forty dollars per person. "Even with the big-time gamblers," my friend went on, "that's a lot of bread off the family table."

Gambling is a universal human activity. Every person seems to have the built-in desire to take a chance and get something for nothing. Scholars would probably dispute the notion that gambling is instinctive, but they would be hard-pressed to deny, the evidence that games of chance seem to pervade every society and intrigue all men. If gambling is an instinct, it must arise from an individual's drive for self-fulfillment. Human potential can never be realized without risk. Growth is not only painful; it is hazardous. Therefore, a person who chooses to grow chooses also the risk of losing. Love itself, then, becomes a gamble. Not only does a person who loves create the potential for his own fulfillment, but he also takes the risk that he may be destroyed. Sound theology would support the axiom, "The greater the love, the greater the gamble." There is a sense in which Christians are called to be the greatest gamblers of all. Jesus actually commended a gambler whose talents paid off ten to one.

Sin is the perversion of a God-given, legitimate desire. When the willingness to take a risk is twisted by the desire to get something for nothing, gambling, then, becomes a sin of perverted stewardship. It is parasitic, producing no personal growth and achieving no social good. Even the strongest advocates of gambling accept the definition that gambling is a nonproductive human activity. It must be justified either by its entertainment value or by the use of its revenues for worthy purposes.

Public opinion about gambling moves in waves. At the present time, there are powerful pressures to make the United States a gambling society with games ranging from church bingo to a nation-wide lottery. The immediate reaction of evangelical Christians is alarm and revulsion. An emotional reaction, however, will not stem the tide. There is a need for facts on which a position can be built. As Chairman of the Governor's *Ad Hoc* Committee on Gambling for the State of Washington, I had to think through a position on gambling in order to defend publicly in the press and on television my minority statement in the Committee's report.

A starting point is to recognize that a scriptural position on gambling must be assumed by inference, not prescription. Arguments based on the stewardship of resources are strong, but they are not conclusive. If affluent Christians evoked the principle of not spending their money except for bread, their conspicuous consumption would make much more sermon material than games of chance in which they do not participate. If the response of Jesus could be second-guessed on the subject, He might have more to say about the stewardship of an affluent church than about the Roman soldiers shooting craps for His clothes at the cross. Ironically, He might point out how the Holy Spirit worked through a game of chance when Matthias was chosen to replace Judas as a disciple.

Why shouldn't Christians gamble? The truth is that

they do. During the mercantile period in the Middle Ages, insurance was invented for merchants who sent their goods to sea against the odds that the ships would be attacked by pirates. Church fathers opposed insurance because God controlled the destiny of ships as well as of men. Insurance was considered not only a lack of faith; it was gambling on the will of God. Yet today, Christians do not consider insurance an "actuarial numbers racket"; it is used as an example of commendable stewardship planning.

Recognizing that the definition of gambling has changed, Christians must currently be concerned about three types of gambling: social gambling, professional gambling, and government gambling. Social gambling emphasizes the entertainment value of games of chance. By legal definition, this means that the participants enter the game on equal terms. There is neither a professional operator, nor a house cut against which the participants have to compete. For example, four friends sit down for an evening of cards in the home of one of the players. Even though the stakes may conceivably rise to thousands of dollars, it is social gambling because the players remain on equal terms. In most instances, this form of gambling is recognized as an individual's privilege.

Social gambling has been extended to organized games, particularly bingo and raffles, as a modest and easily controlled expression of human desire. Sympathy and public pressure, however, identify bingo with charitable and nonprofit institutions, primarily the Roman Catholic Church, which uses the proceeds for religious or charitable purposes. Because of this sympathy and pressure, it can be expected that gambling will be reintroduced to the American public through the door of the church. As a reporter asked me, "Will bingo be the trunk upon which a Christmas tree of gambling is decorated?" With sadness, I had to answer yes.

Gambling in charitable and nonprofit institutions is indefensible for more than the reason that it sets the precedent for other forms of gambling. I have heard the advocates of church bingo oppose state lotteries because the government should not use gambling as a substitute for responsible tax reform. This argument boomerangs on them. It is less defensible to assume that the church can use gambling as a substitute for responsible stewardship than it is for the state to use it as a substitute for responsible taxation. If gambling is a nonproductive human activity, no charitable end will justify the parasitic means!

Professional gambling is a step up from social gambling. The difference is the introduction of a gambling parlor, a professional operator, and what is called a house cut of the proceeds. This is the point at which controls break down and organized crime enters. This kind of gambling is big business and worth the risk of gambling speculators. Their ability to provide the capital for gambling houses, the expertise for professional operators, and the credit to the players cannot be matched. That is just the beginning of the problem. Crime is the intrusion of syndicated interests into gambling; corruption is the bribing of public officials. Crime cannot exist without corruption. Even if there are uniform state laws on gambling, they are effective only if they are enforced. Past experience with the enforcement of gambling laws makes a sordid history. The stakes become so great that enforcement officials can be handsomely paid off as normal expenses for the gambling operation. Crime and corruption, then, increase in direct proportion to the size of the stake and the extent of human involvement. Although public opinion still tends to be negative toward Las Vegas-type slot machines, they are actually easier to control than professional dealers at a card table. Then, the potential for crime and corruption must be joined by the temptation for operators to cheat on individual games. Of all the control problems, this is the most difficult. As an Assistant Attorney General told our Committee, "The possibility of cheating in gambling is limited only by the human imagination."

Few people realize that corruption and cheating plague charitable bingo games as well as professional gambling activities. Charitable bingo is a multimillion-dollar business which requires stringent controls and constant surveillance to keep it honest. Churches must face the question of their responsibility for polluting the moral climate as well as for subverting their principles of stewardship.

If social or professional gambling is inevitable, history dictates the controls that are absolutely necessary to reduce crime, corruption, and cheating. A powerful and independent gambling commission must be created. Uniform state regulations must be adopted which do not permit towns, cities, or counties to set their own rules or choose their own games. Enforcement must come from both state and local levels as a check-and-balance on corruption. Gambling premises, operators, and games must be rigidly screened and licensed to keep out organized crime. Books of the gambling operation must be audited at the point where the money first passes from the player to the operator if skimming of the profits is to be controlled. Penalties on violators must be heavy and automatic. Finally, controls must be set on each type of gambling to minimize cheating by the operators. In short, when the public chooses to gamble, it also chooses for crime, corruption, and cheating. At best, these elements can be reduced, but not eliminated.

Government gambling must be considered by a different set of rules. Statewide lotteries are becoming popular indicators of the public's desire to gamble and the state's need for additional revenues. Arguments in favor of government lotteries usually include the opinion that they are a noncriminal, noncorruptible, noncheating form of entertainment that will produce funds for worthy purposes. In New York State, for instance, the lottery was sold to the public as a means for increasing aid to education. It is true that statewide lotteries are comparatively free from the abuses of social and professional gambling. Other concerns, however, make lotteries a questionable form of government gambling. The basic question is, ''Should the government be involved in gambling?'' Advocates of an affirmative answer will show that most governments are already involved in the promotion as well as the control of certain human vices, such as liquor or horse racing. Those who oppose state lotteries will immediately respond by asking whether the fact of involvement makes it right or whether that involvement should be extended. One thing is certain, when the State becomes a gambling operator with a lottery, the principles of government have to change.

First, the State must promote gambling as a business. Studies of statewide lotteries show that they can succeed only if the State approaches the lottery as a consumer product. In the first year of operation, the lottery revenues are large because of its novelty. At the close of the second year, however, the proceeds are usually cut in half. To avoid some of the loss, the State must keep novelty in marketing the product and must provide improved chances for payout. Frankly speaking, government does not have the market mentality to make the lottery a success.

Second, the entertainment value of lotteries is secondary to the expected increases in revenues. Lotteries may be a convenient and socially acceptable form of gambling for the public, but the major argument is political. They are designed to provide additional revenues in a time of tax rebellion. Yet, a study by the Fund for the City of New York concluded that lotteries were an unreliable source of income. A research analyst put it bluntly, "At its best, a state lottery is good for five or ten years." Not only that, but the start-up costs and the continuing administrative machinery of such a short-term operation make the investment questionable. A well-run lottery will be based upon 45 percent of the revenues for prizes, 40 percent for the State, and 15 percent for administration. It also requires annual betting of eight to ten dollars for every person in the State. Even then, the amount of aid for state treasuries is almost negligible in comparison with the needs. In the State of Washington, for instance, a mathematically designed lottery would provide approximately thirteen million dollars for the State in the first year. This is less than 1 percent of the annual budget. From either the short- or long-range view of revenues, a lottery is difficult to defend.

Third, lotteries are also justified as a means of undercutting the illegal numbers racket. As an admission of the failure of law enforcement, some states have decided to compete with organized crime for the multimillion-dollar gambling market. An assumption is that a legal game will run the lawbreakers out of business. Nothing is further from the truth. To use New York State again as an example, the state lottery has actually been used by organized crime to enhance the numbers racket. In order to obtain the revenues promised for education in the State and still pay out a modest percentage on prizes, the State charges fifty cents for a lottery ticket. The numbers racket, however, only charges twenty-five cents per ticket, provides a more attractive payout, and gives credit to the customers. The fact is that private enterprise, even in gambling, is always more efficient than government bureaucracy.

Many states do not have threatening numbers operations. Therefore, the argument is that a lottery is intended to provide revenues rather than to undercut crime. Initially, this may be the case. Organized crime, however, is interested in extending the tentacles of its influence wherever profits make the venture worthwhile. As a successful competitor with state lotteries, it is possible that a new lottery would actually attract several illegal numbers games. While the advocates of lotteries would call "foul" on this argument, the implications of a decision for a lottery cannot be ignored.

Fourth, a statewide lottery requires the cultivation of a new gambling market. Researchers point out the fact that lotteries are played by middle-class whites rather than poor, black minorities. This finding does not make the lottery a respectable game. The poor minorities can play illegal numbers for one-half the price of the State's ticket, if numbers games are available. If not, the lottery invites the poor to play and it becomes a form of regressive taxation on the poor. In either case, the lottery must be promoted by the creation of new gambling markets. No lottery can succeed on the number of people in the State who already gamble. Young and old, poor and rich, black and white must be counted upon to play the lottery if the operation is to succeed. Then, a greater question arises, "Should the State accept the responsibility for creating a gambling climate?" The implications are far-reaching. Public morality, public safety, and respect for the law suddenly become issues that cannot be avoided. A gambling attitude does affect the quality of life in a state. It certainly would influence the response of people to the claims of Christ. Even evangelism has a stake in the gambling issue. Lotteries are no more innocent than cardrooms or slot machines.

What conclusions can be drawn to guide a Christian's position on gambling?

First, gambling is a vice that violates the principle of Christian stewardship. Although gambling is not specifically prohibited in the Scripture, the nonproductive use of resources, whether money or time, is poor stewardship. Christ said that we would be called to account for the use of our resources, and there is little or no justification for letting chance rule our fortunes for selfish returns when Christ has called us to lose our lives for the sake of the gospel.

Second, if social gambling is inevitable, controls should be demanded to limit crime, corruption, and cheating. Because evangelicals regard gambling as a black-and-white issue, there is a tendency to pull out of the war once the first battle is lost. This is not the time to quit! At the risk of misunderstanding, Christians should call for the controls of an independent gambling commission, uniform state laws, dual enforcement at state and local levels, rigid licensing and standards, and heavy, automatic sanctions on even such innocent games as charitable bingo. The least we can do is make law enforcement workable.

Third, professional gambling should be vigorously opposed by practical as well as moral arguments. Although the public memory is very short, crime, corruption, and cheating accompany professional gambling. Irrefutable evidence also shows the connection between professional gambling and prostitution, drugs, and violence. Once the stakes are high enough, no system of controls can cope with the efficiency, the subtlety, and the daring of organized crime.

Fourth, statewide lotteries are a questionable means for controlling crime or producing state revenues. Under the pretense of satisfying the gambling instincts of respectable citizens, lotteries are political tools to win votes and increase revenues. When a senator announced that the gambling bill in our state would be passed at midnight on the day of the closing legislative session, a knowledgeable newsman told me, "He means that the vote on the gambling bill will be determined by a payoff at midnight." More is at stake than just a lottery for citizens who want to bet. Gambling is a corrupting yeast that contaminates the loaf from core to crust. Christians, who give up when gambling is legalized, will still have to accept the responsibility for the quality of life in their city, county, or state. Even though gambling is wrong, the extent of gambling is still critical.

One lesson stands out from my experience as Chairman of the Gambling Committee. As a Christian, I was overly cautious about being fair. Perhaps I was sensitive to the "Letter to the Editor" that said that the governor's appointment of a minister to Chair the Gambling Committee was like having the pope appoint the devil to guard the holy font. In one sense, my concern for fairness was wise, because I eventually earned the right to speak without being discounted as a minister. The only trouble was that no one else was fair. Flags of vested interests were flown at full mast from the beginning. At one time, the heat of debate produced the veiled threat that the Committee's work was useless anyway, because money and votes would ultimately decide the gambling issue. At any rate, I lost my timidity to speak on moral issues from my convictions as a citizen and as a Christian. In fact, most of the Committee members seemed to be waiting for someone with the nerve to speak with moral conviction.

Whether Christian or not, the roots of our spiritual heritage have not been cut. Christians in the twentieth century can still help keep those roots alive.

QUESTIONS

1. Do you agree that gambling is wrong for a Christian because it is a risk that results in no personal growth, no social good, and no glory to God? If so, are Christians justified to play games of chance when no money is involved? How about putting your name in a box for a supermarket sweepstakes or buying a raffle ticket at the county fair? Is there a Biblical principle to guide us?

2. Not long ago, Christians felt that it was wrong to buy life insurance because Jesus said, "Take therefore no thought for the morrow . . ." (Matt. 6:35). Likewise, they did not invest in the stock market or go into debt because high-risk speculation and high interest rates did not mix with Christian stewardship. Today, adequate insurance, sound investments, and credit buying are accepted and even honored among Christians. Are there Biblical principles to guide us in these matters?

3. The most innocent forms of social gambling are bingo and raffles

conducted to raise funds for charitable organizations, such as churches, lodges, and community associations. Does the good motive modify the moral question about gambling? What if the profits of a state lottery are used exclusively to support educational, cultural, and social improvements? Would you accept public funds from a lottery if you were the president of an eligible educational institution or charitable organization?

4. Evangelical Christians generally seek prohibition against gambling; but if your state or local area already permits some form of gambling, what is the Christian's responsibility—to work to control it and minimize cheating, corruption, and crime? Should a Christian consider a permanent appointment to the commission charged with the control of gambling?

5. The disciples cast lots to choose Matthias to take Judas' place among the twelve (Acts 1:26). Was this a form of gambling condoned by prayer? If not, what was the difference? Does God use chance to achieve His will?

3

O Medical Death,
Where is Thy Sting?

When I was a child, Enoch was my death model. Who can forget the overworked story about God and Enoch walking together one day? Absorbed in conversation, they lost track of time. Dusk settled upon them and God said, "Enoch, we are closer to my home than to yours. Why don't you just come and live with me?" Because there were no boundaries on my childhood dreams, I decided that I too would walk with God and leave this earth like Enoch.

Later on, the purity of my vision of death was tainted by the fantasies of adolescence. David's kingly power in life and death intrigued me. When I read about the beautiful young girl who laid on top of the king in his dying moments, death took on some glamorous overtones. In fact, if you will permit a confession for which I later asked forgiveness, I decided that the David-model of death was not a bad way to go.

Poetry further eased the sting of death for me. In high school, I became a fan of the Romantic poets. Like an eloquent evangelist, I took prizes for reciting such literary gems as Bryant's *Thanatopsis*.

> So live, that when thy summons comes to join
> The innumerable caravan, which moves
> To that mysterious realm . . . approach thy grave
> Like one who wraps the drapery of his couch
> About him, and lies down to pleasant dreams.

If a death trip was necessary, at least I could travel

first class.

Salvation upset my immature, sensual, and romantic death wishes. Isaiah's image of the "Suffering Servant" presented me with a paradox. To follow Christ could mean a horrible death for a glorious cause. Intellectually, I accepted the possibility of a Christlike death as part of my commitment. Emotionally, however, I shrank from its reality. I knew that a lifetime of spiritual growth was ahead of me if I would ever be counted worthy to die as Christ.

In the meantime, I have encountered a new death model that the poets and the prophets never saw. Lacking a better name, I call it the "Medic-model of Death" because it involves Medical Aid, Medical Science, and Medicare.

It all began when a long-distance telephone call interrupted our family dinner. A woman's voice sobbed, "Your father has had a massive heart attack. He was dead, but the Medic crew brought him back." Composed by shock, I asked, "What is the chance for recovery?" The caller answered, "Doctors fear extensive brain damage. He was without oxygen for at least ten minutes."

Part I of the "Medic-model of Death" had unfolded. A Medical Aid crew had saved my father's life. A few years ago, massive heart arrest usually meant certain death because of the time lost between the attack and hospitalization. Mobile medical aid units have reversed the odds. In the first full year of operation in our city, Medic I units saved 66 percent of the heart victims who would have died a few years ago. Mobile units stand ready to respond to emergency calls within five minutes of any place in the city. But what if more than five minutes elapse for a victim who shows no signs of life? Six minutes without oxygen can cripple the brain; eight minutes will extend the damage; and more than ten minutes is hopeless. According to the doctor, my father was without oxygen for ten to twelve minutes!

Moral questions began to surface. If extensive or complete brain damage is certain after eight minutes, how long should emergency treatment continue?

My first answer was easy. I expect a Medic crew to continue life-saving techniques as long as there is any hope. If I had been in the living room of my father's home when the Medics pumped and fibrillated him, I would have begged them, "Keep trying." Brain damage is a risk that I would accept as part of the decision. As emotion drains away, however, my decision changes. If emergency instruments become sophisticated enough to monitor brain damage as well as heartbeat, I would expect a physician to order the crew to stop. In the shock of the moment, a family could not make the decision.

Part II of the "Medic-model of Death" is complicated by the legal implications of advancing medical science. Three doctors tested my father after he was moved to an Intensive Care Unit in the hospital. Unanimously, they concluded that his brain was damaged beyond recovery of either pain or consciousness. Their diagnosis activated a new shock wave. How do you substitute the word "Vegetable" for "Father"? There is a fate worse than death.

Trauma followed trauma. Doctors expected a recurrence of the attack within forty-eight hours. When the deadline passed, the next question was how long life could be sustained on a respirator. Just before the attending physician left for a long weekend, he told me, "On Tuesday, we'll have to make a decision."

Karen Quinlan's case was no longer a distant legal battle headlined in the newspapers. Active euthanasia was no longer a term in a textbook. Karen Quinlan and Loren McKenna had the same progonsis; and the families had the same dilemma, "When do you pull the plug?"

A fighting heart saved us from the decision. To the surprise of the doctors, Dad kicked the respirator by himself. Even without a mind, the will that had guided a strong heart and lungs for sixty-nine years was still programmed to live. Another moral choice was asked of the family. "If the heart stops again, should emergency measures be repeated?" By telephone, the family huddled, prayed and searched for Dad's wishes. We discovered that he had talked of signing a living will which would stipulate that no emergency measure be employed to keep him alive if he was hopelessly ill. Without a dissenting voice, we instructed the hospital to withhold emergency aid if Dad had another attack. Passive euthanasia seemed more tolerable than the act of pulling the respirator plug. But is there really any difference?

Part III of the "Medic-model of Death" was the most torturous because Medicare tangles money with medicine. As my father's condition began to stabilize, life-maintenance measures were taken. Wonder drugs were fed into his system to combat pneumonia, the blood was thinned to remedy clotting, and a transfusion was given to balance internal bleeding. A relative dared to ask, "Why give him blood when it's hopeless?"

Without hearing the question, the doctor responded. His goal was to stabilize the patient's condition so that he could be transferred to a nursing home for custodial care. Failing that, he wanted to keep his patient comfortable and presentable. Skeptically, I queried, "How do you keep a vegetable comfortable?'' Silently, I echoed, ''Why the blood transfusion?'' Perhaps I used the question to beg the truth behind the doctor's plan. Were we ready for the indignity of a prolonged period of living death?

It was time for our lesson in medical economics. A Medicare Review Board in the hospital was making decisions about the level and cost of my father's care. As families of senior citizens are learning, Medicare pays only a portion of medical costs. The hospital must make up the difference from other revenues. Intensive care costs the hospital more than a semi-private room, and a nursing home costs less than a hospital. So, as soon as possible, my father was moved from the costly intensive care unit to a semi-private room. Similarly, as soon as his condition stabilized, he would be moved to a lower cost nursing home.

Medicare has another economic twist for nursing home care. Based upon the average life-expectancy with similar cases, the Medicare Review Board sets an arbitrary limit upon the number of days of full compensation in a nursing home. After that period, the bulk of the cost shifts to the patient and the family. In my father's case, the Review Board set a maximum of twenty days. If his life was prolonged beyond that time, expenses would begin to mount. With this information, came another reason for a living will. In hopeless cases, families are spared excessive costs. Shouldn't living wills limit the use of life-sustaining as well as life-saving measures in hopeless cases?

Our ethical dilemma had now gone full cycle. Starting with the emergency treatment, we asked, ''How long should the Medic crew continue life-saving efforts after oxygen is lost to the brain?'' During intensive care, the decision for active euthanasia was framed by the question,

"If there is no hope, when do you pull the plug?" Regular hospital care flipped the ethical coin, "In the event of another attack, do you plug the respirator in again?" If not, how passive is your mercy? Do you prolong life by nonemergency measures, such as blood transfusions, or do you just keep the dying patient comfortable and presentable? If medical ethics require life-maintenance treatment, is there a reasonable limit of time and cost for the family? By stumbling decisions or standardized ethics, each question was answered as it arrived. For better or worse, only the consequences remained.

Postscript: Almost a month has passed since the attack. My father has remained in the hospital — marginally stable in body, totally senseless in mind. Numbness has now taken over my personal reactions. Initially, I was broken by the news and learned something about myself when my eight-year-old son wept with me, saying, "I've never seen my daddy cry before." Later, I got mad because the attack destroyed my plan to fly my father to my daughter's wedding and our first family reunion in fifteen years. God took the brunt of my rage when I hit the wall and questioned, "Why now?"

Rather than responding to my doubts, God gave me peace. He reminded me that my last words to my father were, "Dad, I love you." Those who have continued to pray for a miracle cannot understand when I say, "Even if Dad should regain consciousness, there is nothing more I need to say to him." Years of spiritual estrangement had been bridged in our last telephone call. With confidence, I knew that the Holy Spirit had followed through.

Guilt came when I had to decide whether to spend the money for a transcontinental trip to visit my father while he was still alive, even though he would not recognize me.

Reason dictated a single trip for the funeral, but emotion does not count the cost. Unspoken resentments were building in relatives at his bedside who grasped the straws of the slightest change as hope that he might have fleeting moments of consciousness. Love, guilt, resentment, and hope all peaked when I was told, "We believe that your father is waiting for his only son before he dies." At midnight, I was on an airplane.

My resentment returned when I saw my father in the hospital. Unseeing eyes, protruding tongue, facial distortions, and animal grunts brought back my experience as a chaplain in a mental ward. My first thought was, "Dad has been turned into a bumbling idiot." Before long, however, my mission was clear. Relatives who had suffered the agony of waiting needed the words and the prayers of a newcomer. Dad also needed me. A three-day beard grizzled his face, totally out of character for my father. It was worth a $400 plane ticket to give him a shave.

On the day that I had to leave him and return home, I awakened in the middle of the night reciting Psalm 121, "I will lift up mine eyes unto the hills, from whence cometh my help. . . ." A Father God was speaking again to a doubting son. In our home, Psalm 121 is known as the "McKenna Psalm." My children have heard the story of their great-grandfather choosing the concluding promise of the Psalm, "The Lord shall preserve thy going out and thy coming in from this time forth, and even for evermore" during devotions on the day of his death. After his funeral, I (as a twelve-year-old boy) drew the same promise when our family gathered to pray. The legacy of that hope, then, has been passed down to my children. As I travel or as married children leave home, the Psalm is

37

recited with our prayers.

In the middle of that last night, I decided that my final devotions at my father's bedside would be to recite the Psalm. Morning came and I went to my Bible to double-check my memory of the words. Flipping the pages of the Old Testament, a yellow tract shaped like a satchel fell out. Unbelievable! Several months earlier I had picked up the tract in a waiting area at O'Hare Field because of its curious shape. (Sooner or later, you find everything and everybody at O'Hare Field.) Inside, there was no evangelistic message, only the words of Psalm 121. I had no idea that I had kept the tract or put it in my Bible!

Before going to the hospital for the last visit, I told my relatives the story, recited the Psalm and prayed. My father's wife said that she had changed her mind and now believed in eternal life. Together we all signed the tract as our commitment and our promise. In the hospital, I taped the tract on the light above my father's head and bent down to whisper, "I will lift up mine eyes unto the hills, from whence cometh my help. My help cometh from the Lord. . . ." Then, with a kiss, I choked, "So long, Buddy; thanks for everything," and raced out to save him the pain of my final tears.

Post-Postscript: A month after his attack and just a few hours after he was moved to a nursing home, my father died. My prayer for mercy was answered and Dad beat the system.

QUESTIONS

1. Medical science has extended the average life-span to seventy-two years for men and seventy-six years for women. What new economic, social, and spiritual problems does this create for elderly people and society in general?
2. What are the advantages and disadvantages of having elderly rela-

tives as members of a family with growing children? Compare these advantages and disadvantages with elderly relatives living in a retirement home.

3. Responsible scientists are concerned about playing God as they anticipate breakthroughs in such areas as genetic engineering to improve the human strain, psychosurgery for emotional problems, creation of life in a test-tube, and transplants of heads as well as hearts. Are there Biblical principles to guide us as man moves into life-and-death questions which were once reserved for the will and act of God?

4. Study a copy of a Christian Living Will. Would you sign it? Why, or why not?

5. More and more life-and-death decisions are being placed in the hands of scientists, medical doctors, and judges, who may or may not include the spiritual dimension in their considerations. Do you think that Christian ministers and counselors should be included, or should we encourage scientists, doctors, and judges who are Christians to get involved? Assume that your local hospital is setting up a panel to review and make recommendations on abortion cases. Would you encourage your minister to be a member?

4

If "R" Is Rotten,
What is "PG"?

I'm mad! In my short saga as a moviegoer, I've trusted the G, PG, R, and X ratings to make decisions for me and my family. No longer. I'm now ready to pour a cup of hemlock for movie moguls who are guilty of corrupting the morals of our young. While I'm at it, I'll also offer a sip to the television tycoons who are slipping sex into daytime serials and vulgarity into Monday through Sunday nine o'clock movies.

To understand my rage, you need to know my moviegoing history. As a preteenager, I lived for Saturday afternoon serials. My sneakered and blue-jeaned gang trouped uptown to see Gene Autrey, Roy Rogers, the Lone Ranger, and The Three Musketeers shoot up the West in the name of justice. Then, just when Hopalong Cassidy was trapped in a badman's hideaway, my parents were converted. As far as I know, Hoppie is still looking down the barrel of a six-shooter fingered by a guy in a black hat.

Seven or eight years later, I tried again. Under pressure from a buddy, I sneaked into a big-band musical when my folks were out of town. As luck (or fate) (or providence) would have it, they cut their trip short, came home early, and found out that I was at the movies. After church the next day, my dad and I went for a long, long drive. Rather than tricking me into lying or charging me with deceit, he simply asked, "How was the show last night?" Nothing more was needed. God had spoken. I stayed out of theaters for six years.

Marriage, middler status in seminary, and friendship with the son of a famous missionary freed me from Dad's taboo. Even though three seminary students had been suspended for attending a movie a year earlier, four of us risked our ministerial careers in a Kentucky movie house. As we sneaked through the lobby after the show, we saw a faculty couple and planned blackmail if they turned us in. On the way home, though, we justified our act by convincing ourselves that "Quo Vadis" was a story with a scriptural basis.

Years later, we joined other faculty couples for "Cinerama Holiday" and Disney's "Davey Crockett." By this time, television was making our living room a theater, and we could catch up with the movies we missed. It was just a matter of time before a movie in a distant city was our "great escape." Once or twice we were embarrassed by the encroachments of some bare skin or dirty words, so we felt morally relieved when movie ratings were introduced. Now I know better. On the basis of my most recent movie experience, I decided that I must return to movie abstinence or fight the ratings. I chose to fight for two reasons.

First, movie abstinence will not cure the same disease that is infecting home television.

Second, Christian youth are going to movies and will continue to go. They may be counting on the ratings to help them make their decisions.

My beef with the media began a week ago. Because I usually get home just long enough to kiss my wife and spank the kids, I started reserving Saturday afternoon to take my six-year-old son swimming. On Friday evening after work, I'd make a big deal of our father-son plans for the next day. For three or four weeks, it worked well. So last Friday night, I bounced into the house, felled my son with a fake karate chop, and gushed, "Hey, Rob, do you know what tomorrow is?"

He answered, "Saturday."

"Right, and do you know what we do on Saturday?"

Rob lapsed into a pensive mood and then spoke with an "I-don't-want-to-hurt-you" tone. "Dad, could I have a day off?"

Out of the mouth of a babe had come the truth. He knew that I was just pretending to enjoy the swimming. But I didn't give up. Casting about for an option, I asked him if he wanted to go to a movie instead. Now *he* was enthusiastic, so I began a search through the movie ads. My teenage daughter told me that "Young Frankenstein" was the fun movie of the season. I checked it out. Because it had a PG — parental guidance — rating, I also read the reviews. "Rich, zany comedy"; "a comic masterpiece" are review comments that I remember. My wife and I then debated the PG rating. We reasoned that the horror parts must have produced the PG rating, but we rationalized that Robbie was already exposed to vampires and werewolves in the Frankenstein reruns that are shown on television after school. What could be better? Saturday afternoon with the family — father, mother, and son — watching "Young Frankenstein" *together*.

The theater was a screaming, swirling mass of popcorned and Milk-Dudded kids. Quiet came only when the movie began. Within a matter of minutes, I knew that the feelings of the movie affected the kids, but the words were for parents. To demonstrate an involuntary reflex, Dr. Frankenstein faked a kick to the victim's crotch. Breasts and bedding were soon established as the focus of the fun for the "comedy of the year." My wife and I debated leaving the theater, but we again reasoned that the double entendre script was beyond the six-year-old mind. Insults to our intelligence and infringements upon our values continued until the end when Dr. Frankenstein and his creation exchanged not only brains but other monstrous parts. Before it was over, sex acts were flaunted, religion was debased, and God's name was taken in vain. Today's PG film was yesterday's advanced R rating.

Self-righteous readers are already asking, "Why didn't you walk out?" I would have, except that I figured my six-year-old missed the gross comedy. Later on, I wished that I had, so that my son would know that his dad was capable of moral rage, even when the boy didn't know why. It's too late now, but I can still learn lessons.

Four vows came out of that movie experience. *First,* I will not take my children to another PG movie, even though I cannot always protect them from PG television.

Second, I will sharpen my moral sensitivity to the occasional movies I attend or watch in my home.

Third, I will call for evangelical Christians to protest the moral slippage in movie and television ratings. By the time this column is printed, the annual convention of the National Association of Evangelicals will have been held in Los Angeles, California. What better place than Hollywood's backyard to raise a powerful evangelical voice against the political and economic forces which are playing fast and loose with American morals? As a companion to this column, I will present a resolution of protest against the ratings and call for evangelical input.

Fourth, if the movie-raters and television-coders do not respond, perhaps evangelical Christianity needs a morality rating of its own for movies and television in a weekly or monthly Christian periodical.

Some would complain that this is a return to the soul-stifling *Index* of the Roman Catholic Church. Others would claim a moral breakdown in evangelical convictions when it is assumed that Christians attend movies and their appetites are whetted for the forbidden fruit of R- and X-rated movies. Let's face it. Most evangelical Christians are seeing movies of questionable moral value — either at home or in the theater. Therefore, if we cannot change the moral standards of the movie industry or set our own standards, we must teach our people to make value judgments consistent with biblical principles. At this time, I see no one rushing to lift the standard. Who'll be first?

QUESTIONS

1. Is the careful selection of movies an alternative to complete prohibition or complete freedom for Christians? If so, what standards would be applied for deciding which movies to attend?

2. What are the pros and cons of the church taking responsibility to review and recommend movies, television programs, drama, and books for Christians? How would you implement such a proposal? Would it infringe upon the freedom of Christians to make mature decisions?

3. Boycotts of movies and television have been tried by church groups. Are they effective? If not, what better method for influencing the quality of programming would you propose?

4. When he reaches the age of eighteen, an average child will have spent 16,000 hours before the television set. How can a Christian family regulate these hours, provide creative options for television time, and even use television for teaching moral development and Christian values?

5. A leading educator has said that television has more impact upon taste and values than the home, school, or church. If so, are relig-

ious telecasts enough? How would you creatively use a thirty-second spot during the commercials to communicate Christ and Christian values?

5

How About the Victims in No-Fault Divorce?

Evangelicals may be sleeping through another revolution. While debating inerrancy, opposing church unity, and passing resolutions for bluenosed laws, the ethical foundations of our legal system are being replaced. "No-fault" laws are replacing sanctions on individual behavior. "Victimless" crimes are changing the standards of right and wrong. In law, it appears as if we are sacrificing justice in order to avoid injustice. But in doing that, we are also trading the theological concept of original sin for the romantic concept of original genius. Soon, we may live in a legal jungle where victimless crime is unpunished, and consenting adults have no fault.

One-step marriage and no-fault divorce laws are the latest additions to the legal revolution. The National Commission on Uniform Laws has proposed that all states adopt a revised code on marriage and divorce with some basic changes that are both legal and theological.

First, it is proposed that marriage be a civil contract without the need for solemnization. Traditionally, marriage has been considered a two-step process with civil and religious ceremonies. A couple had the option of solemnizing their marriage before a civil official rather than a minister, but even then, the ceremony was quasi-religious. The underlying assumption was that marriage had a spiritual as well as a legal component that should be recognized. Now, the proposal is to limit the legal language to civil registration by making solemnization optional. Marriage would be a "paper" contract without the trappings of moral vows. It would pave the way for an "easy in-easy out" marriage and divorce system in our society.

Second, a uniform no-fault divorce system is proposed. A marriage contract may be dissolved when a marriage is irretrievable. The wording is significant. "Divorce" carries with it the trauma and stigma of broken vows and shattered relationships. Therefore, the word "dissolution" is substituted in order to connote a mutual agreement on canceling the marriage contract.

"Irretrievability" is then introduced as a substitute for the "adversary" system in divorce proceedings. Now, one partner must be found at fault in the divorce decision as a basis for alimony, property disposition, and child custody. This requires that a husband and wife become adversaries by charges and countercharges. Consequently, the courts themselves become part of the wedge that is driven between partners. Any chance that the couple had for reconciliation when the divorce proceedings began is lost in the need to escalate the accusations in order to win the case. In the proposed system, the need to prove fault is eliminated. If, by mutual arrangement of the partners, or in the opinion of the court, the marriage is irretrievable, the contract may be dissolved.

Third, maintenance (alimony) and property disposition are determined by the financial condition of the partners, rather than by a court decision on guilt or innocence. The same is true of child custody. Within the best of its knowledge, the court makes custody provisions in the interest of the child, rather than in the interest of the "winner" in the divorce. In the wording of the proposed law, it is stated that maintenance, property disposition, and child custody shall be established without regard for marital misconduct on the part of husband or wife. "Marital misconduct" is a sanitized word for adultery, cruelty, and desertion. It is necessary, however, to be consistent with a no-fault divorce system.

Fourth, a proposal for a family court undergirds the one-step marriage and no-fault divorce laws. The emphasis is upon marriage counseling rather than upon adversaries in court. Provision is made for a "cooling off" period after the divorce papers are filed. During this time, the family court enters the scene. A couple is asked to appear before the court and enter a counseling relationship. If either partner refuses counseling, the court can make a decision about irretrievability. Hopefully, the couple may find some threads to keep the marriage together. If not, it is hoped that an agreement can be reached on alimony, property, and children — without bitterness and disillusionment. At the present time, family courts exist as experimental projects with the possibility of rapid expansion in the future.

Fifth, the proposed laws also declare all children as legitimate. This is an enlightened view in which children do not have to bear the label of illegitimacy as well as live with the handicap of an incomplete home. It has long been said that there are no illegitimate children, only illegitimate parents. The new law makes this adage a legal fact.

Scriptural teaching and Christian tradition are in conflict with the major assumptions behind these laws. Marriage is recognized in the Scriptures as a spiritual relationship as well as a public statement. Proponents of the new laws will be quick to say that a religious ceremony is still an option for any couple. The larger

49

question, however, is the secularization of the law as a part of a trend to separate our society from its religious roots. The present system also provides an option for the nonreligious couple who do not want to solemnize their marriage before a clergyman. Perhaps, in the spirit of the Constitution, the law should be secular with the religious option, rather than religious with a secular choice. The danger is in the intangible fear that our nation will forget God when we rebuild our legal foundations on the assumption that He does not exist.

Another dilemma is the conflict between the evils of the current divorce system and the recognition of the biblical basis for divorce. Christ made adultery the condition of divorce. Interpreted literally, it supports the "adversary" concept of charges and countercharges. Yet, Christ made it clear that adultery was forgivable and that people were more important than the laws. At present, our divorce laws are legalistic. Justice is more important than mercy. Now, the proposed laws are heavily weighted toward mercy without the provision for grace. Humanistic and secular motives dictate the change. In typical human fashion, the swing is from justice without mercy to mercy without justice. It is another case in which evangelical Christians rested in the assumption that our laws are based on compatible religious principles rather than taking a creative and scriptural view of a human problem. Now, it is too late. No-fault divorce laws are inevitable. Therefore, our only option is to speak publicly on behalf of the spiritual as well as the legal commitment in marriage, to renounce sin as well as to offer forgiveness in marriage relationships, and to offer religious counseling as a part of the reconciliation or separation process of the family court.

Our concern should also extend to the broader question of a society based on no-fault laws. A sense of sin can be personally devastating, but it is also necessary for a man to know his need for God. Informally, a no-fault attitude already exists among the young. Sin has given way to cultural disadvantage or a different style of life. The impact of a legalized no-fault law may make it more difficult to convince men of their sin, or it may give the church an unusual opportunity to respond to a sense of personal rather than institutional sin. Although the full implications are still unknown, it is possible the ethical revolution toward a no-fault society may be an alarm clock for a sleeping church.

QUESTIONS

1. Which is more important, the sacredness of the marriage vow or the happiness of the individual? Can these two extremes be reconciled?

2. A sociologist once noted that when 50 percent of all marriages end in divorce, the quality of American life as we have known it will be lost. Do you agree? What are some of the social repercussions of a rising divorce rate?

3. Divorce impacts a church with single divorced members, remarried couples, and combinations of first, second, and even third marriages. What are the special needs of these people? How can the church minister to their needs and those of their children through its identification as the extended family of God?

4. At one time, churches held stringently to the idea that adultery was the only legitimate reason for a divorce; now, other grounds are cited for justification. Is there a Biblical basis for irreconcilable differences as a reason for divorce? Should the standards for divorce differ between Christian and non-Christian?

5. Jesus said that divorce was permitted by the Law because of the hardness of the people's hearts. What did He mean? Does the same

indictment apply to the divorce problem today? If you were asked to develop a special ministry of the church to prevent divorce, what would you propose?

6

Do the Unborn
Need a Bill of Rights?

Abortion! A word that strains medical knowledge, tests legal limits, provokes theological debate, and prompts marches on the White House. The full force of the issue is being felt as Congress is caught in the cross fire of emotion over the constitutional amendment guaranteeing "the right to life." There is often more heat than light in the battles between the proponents of "no abortion" with major representation from the Roman Catholic community and the advocates of "abortion by demand" represented by the Women's Liberation Movement. In between is a compromise position which permits "abortion by prescription," when the life of the mother is in danger or the pregnancy is the result of rape or incest.

Evangelical Christianity's response to abortion has been the sound of silence, punctuated by a few moralistic thunderings. Yet, students of the abortion issue indicate that the major conflict is between the theological principle of the sacredness of human life (that has been translated into law) and the individual rights of the woman to determine if and when she shall bear a child. Perhaps the lack of a specific biblical perspective on abortion has caused evangelical Christians to forfeit the debate to the Roman Catholics and liberal Protestants. Or, perhaps evangelical Christians are still entertaining the assumption that we live in a Christian culture where morality is legislated by laws derived from the majority's theological position. Either of these reasons is preferable to the accusation that evangelical Christians prefer the status quo of anti-abortion laws so that they can maintain the double standard of a conservative public stance, but liberal private practice. This is too harsh an indictment. The silence of evangelical Christians on abortion reform is probably the absence of a biblical directive and the lack of information on a complex social issue which requires a moral decision between two greater goods or two lesser evils.

The Abortion Questions

The primary question about abortion is theological. "What is the nature and the value of human life?" The Christian answer is that man was created by God as a living soul in His own image. Thus, the nature of human life is eternal and its value is sacred. From this position, both a positive and negative approach to abortion has been developed. The positive approach is to hold life so sacred that only God can begin or end it. In respect for its sacredness, a woman will bear a child even when the child is unwanted or the life of the mother is in danger. The doctrine of the sacredness of life also implies protección of the weak, including the unborn as well as those who are born deformed, retarded, despised, or impoverished. Conservative Roman Catholics hold this position so strongly that they maintain that liberalized abortion laws will cheapen human life and permit genocide in such forms as sterilization and euthanasia. They argue that liberalized abortion laws would only "transfer the execution chamber to more aseptic conditions."

Responsibility to maintain the sacredness of human life is the positive side of the Christian doctrine on the nature and value of man. The negative aspect is punishment for violations against the sanctity of human life. Premarital and extramarital sex relations are sins for which the sinner must bear the consequences. Therefore, if the laws are liberalized so that an unwanted child can be aborted by a mother's demand or a doctor's recommendation, another social sanction against a form of sin has been erased. Exponents of this position go so far as to say that a young girl who is pregnant by rape or incest should bear the child because of the sacredness of the life principle and in order to avoid opening the door for other exceptions. At the farthest end of this extreme position is the belief that the Christian link between suffering and perfection applies in these circumstances.

Beyond the theological principle of the sacredness of human life, questions about abortion are derived from a mixture of biology, ethics, medicine, law, and sociology. The biological question is, "When does human life begin?" Views vary from the Roman Catholics who hold that life and soul begin at conception to the Jews who believe that human life begins at birth. In between is the evidence of the quickening of the fetus and the time that it can survive independent of the mother. Evangelical Christians tend to take the intermediate position, at least, in the practice of certifying birth and holding funerals. This means that a distinction has been made between *potential* human life and *actual* human life. Therefore, an ethical question is raised, "What is the hierarchy of values by which moral decisions are made in favor of the higher good?" More specifically, "Is the living mother more important than the unborn child?" and "Is *actual* human life more important than *potential* human life in fetal development?"

Once the door of the moral dilemma is open, there is no end to the questions. The easy retreat is to go back to the sovereignty of God by relinquishing moral responsibility for decision-making. The realistic approach, however, is to recognize that when God told man to "Be fruitful, and multiply, and replenish the earth" (Genesis 9:1), He brought him into a partnership in creation. This was not just an invitation to a never-ending population explosion; it was also a commission to be responsible for His creation and to judge it against the standard that God used when He said, "It is good" (Genesis 1:31). Therefore, the question of abortion must be extended to its medical, legal, and sociological aspects. Medical doctors are pledged to the preservation of life; but they must face the question: "When is the physical life of my patient in danger so that I must choose between lives and abort the child or lose the mother?" *Liberalized abortion laws extend the power of the physician to decisions beyond the life and death of the mother to the physical and mental health of both mother and child.*

The legal question adds more confusion to the issue. A powerful force behind the drive to liberalize abortion laws is the individual right of a woman to determine if and when she wants to be a mother. This is a stand against the position that the right to determine life belongs either to God or to society as represented by physicians, fathers, or panels of experts. It holds that a woman is not a chattel of a male or Protestant-dominated culture; she is an individual with the full rights of self-determination. The only problem is that when the courts support this drive for the privacy and rights for the individual woman, they are also supporting them for the individual unborn child! This poses the legal question of abortion: "Whose rights are more important —the mother's, or the unborn, living child's?"

To cap off the confusion, the ecological problem of overpopulation must be considered. If the "no abortion" stance is taken, it includes a commitment to maintain the quality of life among the masses as well as a belief in the checks and balances of natural population controls. If the "abortion by demand" position is taken, it implies that abortion is a back-up for contraception and may suggest social legislation on other kinds of population controls. In either case, the question is: "Which is more important — controls on population, or protection of the individual woman's right to decide if, when, and how many children she will bear?"

The Abortion Options

Out of this collection of beliefs, facts, and values, three positions have emerged. "No abortion" is the most conservative position. It is based upon the theological principle that only God has the right to determine life, if the sacredness of human life is to be maintained. This position is beginning to emerge in public consciousness as cars are carrying the placard, "This Family Believes That Abortion Is Murder." The inherent weaknesses of the position are evident in its theoretical vagueness and practical inconsistency. It is difficult to argue against the doctrine of the sacredness of life, particularly if you are a Christian. But, it is equally difficult to argue that a change in the abortion law is categorically murder and that it sets the precedent for population control by genocide. In practice, the argument loses more strength when the exponents of this position hold that any kind of abortion is murder but will defend the concept of the "just

57

war." The final stroke, however, is the evidence that most states already permit therapeutic abortion when the life of the mother is in danger. To accept this position is to admit that there are conditions for "just abortion."

The other extreme position is "abortion by demand." As the "no abortion" stance is based upon the theological principle of the sanctity of human life, this position is based upon the principle that "no unwanted or unintended child should ever be born.'' The premium is upon individual rights and happiness. God and society have been removed from the scene, and the responsibility rests solely with the mother-to-be. The weaknesses of this position are written in the loss of the spiritual and social values which undergird our society. Individual happiness is more important than the sacredness of human life. Individual decisions are more important than social responsibility. The individual rights of the mother are more important than the legal rights of the unborn child. As its opposite extreme, this option loses strength in practical contradictions. For instance, exponents of abortion by demand also tend to be the advocates of social legislation for compulsory population controls. At the same time that they call for the uncomplicated abortion of human life in the fetus, they will march in protest against killing by war, capital punishment, pollution, or over-population.

The compromise position of "abortion by prescription" is complicated by even finer lines of moral distinction. At the present time, the laws in most states permit therapeutic abortion when the life of the mother is in danger. The question is how far we will go with a justifiable prescription for abortion. The scale of conditions for which abortion might be prescribed includes pregnancies which may result in:

1. Death of the mother.
2. Physical illness or deformity of the mother or child.
3. Illegitimate birth as a result of rape, incest, or other felonious intercourse.
4. Mental illness of mother or child.
5. Loss of social or economic well-being for the family.
6. Illegitimate birth as a result of premarital or extramarital sex relations without the possibility of marriage.
7. Birth of an unwanted child by a married woman.

Generally speaking, the advocates of abortion by prescription have proposed laws that permit abortion for the first four conditions on the scale. The Model Penal Code proposes abortion in cases when the physical or mental health of the mother is at stake, when the child may be born with a physical or mental defect, and when the pregnancy is the result of rape, incest, or other felonious intercourse. In recent days, Billy Graham has taken a public position in general support of abortion under these conditions. The Christian Medical Society has also taken a similar position, although the exact details are not spelled out in either case.

Abortion by prescription puts a heavy weight of responsibility on the spiritual and social integrity of its advocates. Theological critics will find an element of situational ethics in the position. Legal critics will maintain that rights of the woman are even more proscribed by a jury of experts who are called upon to make the decision. Yet, in the contemporary climate of weakening theological certainties, increasing social pluralism, and rising individual rights, new and liberalized abortion laws will be enacted. It is only a matter of time and content.

An Abortion Stance

Options for the church on the abortion issue have been described in *The Religious Situation, 1968* by Ralph B. Potter, Jr.

> The church may: (1) reinforce its theological position against abortion; (2) adopt the "abortion by demand" position with a radical change in its theological position; (3) split its position with a "Christian" view for church and "secular" view for the larger public; or (4) adopt the "abortion by prescription" position and share responsibility for prescribing and managing those conditions.

The same options apply to evangelical Christianity. In fact, there would be very few evangelicals who would not recommend abortion if the life of the mother is in danger. Pragmatically, there are also very few evangelical Christians who would oppose abortion for a girl who was a minor and had been raped. The consent of silence of evangelical Christianity on The Pill is another indicator of our predisposition to abortion by prescription, because many of the same issues apply to birth control as well as to abortion.

If abortion by prescription is supported by intelligent action rather than by default, evangelical Christianity has some new responsibilities.

First, there must be a strengthening of the doctrine of the sacredness of life. Abortion by prescription does not cancel out this doctrine. It demands a sharpening of the principle and its application in specific situations.

Second, there must be up-to-date research on the issue of abortion in relation to Christian values. The columnist who reported on Billy Graham's position on abortion said that the evangelist needs a research team to give his public pronouncements on social and political issues the perspective of human knowledge as well as the biblical truth. This recommendation should be considered by every evangelical Christian organization and church. A biblical perspective on ethical issues is a survival need and a moral responsibility of Christians today. The research centers already exist in the Christian college if the church and related organizations would charge them with this responsibility and then give them the financial and moral support to deal with these delicate issues.

Third, informed evangelical Christians must accept responsibility for helping shape public policy on abortion. Because legislation is a product of political compromise, vested interests are already pressing their claims. Crusaders for abortion by demand are campaigning with a concept of human life that is thoroughly naturalistic. Liberal theologians are proposing reforms that apply the love ethic to the whole of society. Medical doctors are claiming that the abortion decision is exclusively their prerogative. Jurists are weighing the constitutional freedoms of the born and the unborn from the legal perspective of history and practice. Meanwhile, politicians are watching the scene with one eye on their responsibility and the other on the polls. Evangelical Christians are obligated to enter this debate with the strength of the doctrines of creation, the sacredness of life, and the spiritual responsibility of man. The "salt of the earth" is the parable of involvement in the abortion issue.

Fourth, evangelical Christians must make moral decisions on the conditions for abortion that are based upon the values which are supported, but not necessarily specified, by the Scriptures. For instance, the sacredness of life is more important than happiness. Personal health is a higher value than personal convenience. An innocent victim should be considered before a consenting participant. The present killing of a life is less moral than the prediction of a future mutilation of the spirit.

These value choices will create controversy in themselves. But, when the decision maker takes the risk of supporting a specific policy, he will alienate some and be misunderstood by many. At that time, he must stand upon his understanding of God's Word, his discernment of the Spirit, his knowledge of the issue, and his conviction that Christian involvement is better than neutrality.

Fifth, evangelical Christians must be willing to participate in the decisions on specific cases regarding abortion. Many of the abortion reform bills put the power for decision making in the hands of a panel that may include physicians, psychiatrists, social case workers, lawyers, and clergymen. Because of the importance of the abortion issue and its ramifications for Christian influence in the society, evangelicals in each of these professions should be demanding that the legislation make provision for a broad-based decision by a panel of experts. Clergymen, in particular, should be included on the consulting team. It is not only an opportunity to maintain a spiritual influence in the life-and-death decisions of a changing society; but it is the opportunity for a ministry where confused values, personal guilt, and interpersonal conflict are not resolved by surgical techniques or legal decisions.

Sixth, and finally, the call to the involvement of evangelical Christians in the abortion issue includes the need for a specific statement of reform. On the basis of the information and the opinions that have already been expressed, legislation could be supported with these provisions:

1. A preamble statement regarding the divine gift of human life, its sacredness, and man's responsibility to hold the preservation of life as one of our highest moral values.
2. A statement indicating that therapeutic abortion may be legally considered only for the most compelling reasons and by individual cases.
3. The requirement that the woman be a resident of the state for at least ninety (90) days.
4. The requirement that therapeutic abortion be permitted only with the prior consent of the woman, her husband or legal guardian, and with the consultative opinion of a panel of resource experts including such persons as a physician, a psychiatrist, a lawyer, a social worker, and a clergyman.
5. The provision that the conditions for abortion be limited to the preservation of the physical or mental health of the mother or child and in cases where pregnancy is the result of rape, incest, or other felonious intercourse.
6. The requirement that the pregnancy be terminated no more than four months after the date of conception.
7. The requirement that the termination of pregnancy be performed in an accredited medical facility by a licensed physician.
8. The statement that physicians as well as patients are protected against unwillful participation in induced abortion.
9. The declaration of the rights of the unborn living child after four months and of the infant after birth, with infanticide a crime under all circumstances.

The conclusion must be a note of irony. After labored efforts to understand the abortion issue and to take a position, the whole problem may be academic. It is predicted that an abortifacient pill will be perfected within a few years that will make the contraceptive pill obsolete and also make abortion by demand a right that will be conferred upon women by scientific advancement. When that time comes, evangelical Christians will not be concerned with social sanctions, medical techniques, and legal interpretations. The issue then will be the extent to which the sacredness of human life and the weight of moral responsibility has been written upon the "fleshly tables of the heart" (II Corinthians 3:3) rather than in the laws of the land.

QUESTIONS

1. What are the pros and cons of the government providing free abortions for women who have been raped or whose lives are endangered by pregnancy? Which position would you take?

2. Christians who oppose abortion sometimes face personal situations which test their principles. For instance, would you consider an abortion for an unwed daughter? If she were underage? If the father were of a different race? If she were raped? What values would guide your decision in each case?

3. If your daughter had a baby out of wedlock and the father was unknown would you recommend that she keep the baby or put it out for adoption? Why?

4. How is the moral issue of abortion related to contraception at the beginning of life and to mercy-killing at the end of life? If we lose the "right to life" in one area, do we endanger the others?

7

Is Punishment by Death a Capital Idea?

Five men on death row awaited execution in the electric chair. Joe's number came up first. As he started the shuffling steps in the last mile, he passed the cell of the fourth condemned man who whispered, "Good-bye, Joe." A few more steps and the third prisoner choked out, "So long, Joe." And then the second was heard to weep, "Farewell, Joe." At a loss for words, and wanting to cut the gloom of the moment, the last inmate grasped the bars of his cell and blurted out, "More power to you, Joe." Have we too, run out of good words to the man on death row?

Capital punishment is not dead. The issue seethes in courts and legislatures at both federal and state levels. As usual, the debate is complicated by theological and sociological questions as well as by legal decisions and political pressures. Battle lines were drawn when the Supreme Court followed the trend toward the protection of individual rights and ruled against capital punishment. In a controversial 5-4 decision, the Court said that capital punishment as now administered violates the Eighth and Fourteenth Amendments because it "constitutes cruel and unusual punishment." While the ruling spared the lives of six hundred persons who were awaiting death in thirty-one states, it opened the door for a return to the death penalty for specific cases when it can be shown that the conviction is not arbitrary or capricious and, therefore, not "cruel and unusual."

Politically, the climate is mixed between the Court's concern for the rights of criminals as persons and the public's concern for public safety. A majority of Americans give support to recent legislation and enforcement actions that have been taken to curb crime. Even the latest statistics which show the first reduction in the crime rate in seventeen years are used to support this attitude because the statistics can be used to show that the "get tough" policies are working. Responding to the mind-set of the "New Majority," the Nixon administration called for legislative action on the first revision of the Criminal Code since 1709. The proposal includes the death penalty in cases of war-related crimes, such as treason; killing of law-enforcement officials; and murders connected with federal crimes, such as hijacking. After a defendant has been convicted of one of these crimes, however, the jury must also decide whether there are mitigating or aggravating circumstances which may affect the conviction. A defendant's life would be spared if there are mitigating circumstances, and the death penalty would be mandatory if the circumstances were aggravating. Even with these provisions, constitutional attorneys question whether capital punishment will be reinstated by the Supreme Court. At any rate, a head-to-head confrontation between the executive and judicial branches of government is predicted.

Criminologists cannot be neglected when capital punishment is discussed. As they see the issue, it is a matter of deterrence versus rehabilitation. If it could be shown that capital punishment were an effective instrument for deterring or reducing capital crimes, criminologists would support it. The evidence, however, is not conclusive. In fact, it is weighted against capital punishment as a deterrent. Most violent crimes which could lead to the death penalty are episodic and irrational. "Episodic" means that the chances are very slim that the person who committed the crime would ever face the same circumstances again; "irrational" means that the defendant was temporarily or permanently insane. The question then centers upon criminals who deliberately commit major crimes and upon cases in which national security or public safety are jeopardized. Some criminologists take the position that capital punishment should be retained for these specific situations. Still, as advocates of prison reform, they have a prior commitment to the rehabilitation of criminals. Capital punishment has a finality that eliminates all future alternatives. This, criminologists argue, is contradictory to our appellate court system and our respect for human rights. Once a person is dead, errors in legal judgment cannot be corrected, new evidence cannot be introduced, and the chance for change in human behavior cannot be contemplated. Someone has to play God with a human life. Therefore, as long as there is a chance of error, new evidence, or rehabilitation, the death penalty fails on both legal and humanitarian grounds.

Theological arguments inevitably creep into the scene. When the proponents of capital punishment want to bring a moral weapon into the battle, they quote the principle of *lex talionis* in the Old Testament, "An eye for an eye, a tooth for a tooth," and escalate its meaning to "A life for a life." In criminology, this is commonly called "cash register justice" or letting the punishment fit the crime. Old Testament scholars, however, refute this extended interpretation. They say that the original purpose of the talion principle was to provide compensation for the victims of crime rather than to justify the death penalty. How the cycle turns! Our legislatures are just now considering society's responsibility to the victims of crime — an Old Testament principle of 2000 B.C.!

A more accurate expression of Old Testament justice might be the commandment, "Thou shalt not kill." It is clearly a personal commandment, but does it also apply to the State or to an agent of the State? Paul, in the thirteenth chapter of Romans, made the agent of the State also the agent of God for justice and retribution. If his position is accepted, there are different standards for personal and public justice. Paul does not go so far as to specify capital punishment, but it can be implied from the words, "But if thou do that which is evil, be afraid; for he beareth not the sword in vain: for he is a minister of God, a revenger to execute wrath upon him that doeth evil" (v. 4).

Jesus added another dimension to the theological implications of capital punishment when he said, "Ye have heard that it hath been said, An eye for an eye, and a tooth for a tooth: But I say unto you, That ye resist not evil: but whosoever shall smite thee on thy right cheek, turn to him the other also" (Matthew 5:38-39). His standard went far beyond the claim of Old Testament justice in which compensation, equal to the loss, is made to the victim. *persuing this*

But Jesus called His followers to demonstrate the meaning of love by compensating the criminal! If this standard is harked back to the question of capital punishment, there seems to be a quality of mercy implied that makes it difficult for a Christian to take a stance for the death penalty without reservation. A former question returns: "Is the biblical standard of justice for an individual different than it is for the State?" Now, that question is joined by another: "Is the biblical standard of mercy for a redeemed person different than the standard for an unredeemed person?" In other words, does the perversity of man and society require justice even though Christians are called to live by grace? If the answer is yes, then some form of capital punishment might be advocated as consistent with a theology of justice for an unredeemed society.

Out of this maze of legal, political, sociological, and theological arguments, it is difficult to frame a single and unflexing position. We do, however, know the most important questions:

1. Do criminals have a right to live despite the crime they have committed?
2. Can the legal process provide adequate protection against arbitrary and capricious decisions for the death penalty?
3. Is capital punishment a deterrent to capital crime?
4. Is an individual who chronically and rationally commits capital crimes past the point of rehabilitation?
5. Are there certain specific crimes that are related to national security or public safety which justify the death penalty?
6. Is the State a person to which the biblical standards of justice apply?
7. Is the State an agent of God for justice, including retribution?
8. Does the Bible imply different standards of justice and mercy for individuals and the State?
9. Does the Bible imply different standards of justice and mercy for redeemed and unredeemed persons?

As a Christian grappling with these questions and seeking the guidance of the Holy Spirit, my tentative response would be to advocate the death penalty for those persons convicted of capital crimes by habit or profession and for those who endanger national security or public safety in committing those crimes. Examples would be paid killers, cop killers, spy killers, and hijack killers. An essential qualifier for the proposal would be the requirement that the jury take into consideration mitigating or aggravating factors that would prohibit the death penalty or make it mandatory. From a legal standpoint, this position assumes that individual rights have a limit and that, despite the human factor in the legal process, there are times when sufficient evidence warrants the finality of the death penalty. Sociologically, it strikes a balance between the extremes of deterrence and rehabilitation. Deterrence by death may not be proven, but neither is rehabilitation by custody. For certain criminals and certain crimes, justice dictates death. Theologically, a distinction is drawn between the responsibility of individuals and the State. In their interpersonal relationships, Christians must be ruled by the law of love. Justice, however, must rule the State as a part of the check-and-balance system on human nature. Therefore, the State is the agent of God for justice while the Church is the agent for redemption. Capital punishment becomes the extreme form of justice that the State will use as infrequently as possible in order to maintain the system of justice.

Uneasy rests the head that dares to wear a moral crown. My tentative position seems reasonable, but it does not feel right. I continue to ask, "Is capital punishment justice or revenge?" "Is a person ever past the point of no return?'' ''Is love the mitigating factor that should always put the Christian on the side of forgiveness?'' ''Can God's purpose to justify men be best demonstrated by Christians who take a position for justice or mercy on the issue of capital punishment?''

As the struggle continues, tomorrow's answer may be different.

QUESTIONS

1. Conservative Christians are often aligned with advocates of capital punishment. Can Christians be theologically conservative and socially liberal with regard to such questions as capital punishment?

2. Courts are supposed to make impartial judgments on social problems. If so, how do you account for the fact that the Supreme Court rulings on capital punishment seem to have moved from left to right along with the conservative trends in American public opinion? Does the law change with the times?

3. The sacredness of human life is a Biblical principle which seems to conflict with the need for public safety in the question of capital punishment. Are there conditions when public safety supersedes an individual's right to live? What guidance does the Bible give us on this question?

4. Justice and mercy are two sides of the same coin in Christian responsibility. Is there a way in which both of these requirements can be preserved in a position on capital punishment?

5. The talion principle, ''Eye for eye, tooth for tooth . . .'' (Exod. 21:24), has been used to justify capital punishment. Is this interpretation of the Old Testament Law correct? How is the principle fulfilled, not destroyed, in the teachings of Christ? On which side of capital punishment do you think Christ would stand if He were asked the question today?

8

Why Aren't Christians
in Jail Where They Belong?

If he had shouted or sworn, I could have turned him off; but the black man just drilled me with his eyes and said, "Unless something is done right away, there will be more Atticas."

The prison riot of Attica was another blot on the record of American democracy. Whatever the cause, and however it was handled, Attica joins Dallas, Watts, Kent State, and Vietnam on a list of names that we wish we could forget.

A prison riot poses a particular problem for evangelical Christians. The Scriptures say little or nothing about political assassinations, racial violence, or campus revolt. Prisons and prisoners, however, are cited time and again as a specific social responsibility for the followers of Christ. In the first sermon that He preached, Jesus said that He was "anointed . . . to preach deliverance to the captives" (Luke 4:18). His words might have to be interpreted as a metaphor for the "prisoner of sin," except that He also included prisons and prisoners in the final judgment test. If Matthew 25 is taken literally, there are few evangelical Christians who would want to have their eternal destiny turn on Jesus' words, "I was in prison, and ye came unto me" (Matthew 25:36). The apostle writers, however, took these words seriously. The writer of the Hebrews said, "Think constantly of those in prison as if you were prisoners at their side" (Hebrews 13:3, Phillips).

Christianity is a religion with a long prison record. That may be why visiting those in prison is singled out as one of the unavoidable commandments for Christian social action. John the Baptist ended his career under the shadow of doubt that only a prisoner knows. He sent his disciples to Jesus to ask, "Are you the one who was to come or are we to look for somebody else" (Matthew 11:3, Phillips)? Jesus himself had a short, but humiliating, prison record. In the book of Acts, for instance, a prison record is almost a badge of apostleship. Paul set an early record for Christian incarceration when he waited three or more years for his trial before Caesar. Even though he carried on a ministry in prison, the bright notes of his prison letters are found in the letters, the visits, the packages, and the aid of his friends and fellow apostles. It should be no surprise, then, that the New Testament ends with the vision of a prisoner. John, in the exile on Patmos, saw heaven and left us a picture of God's view of the future.

A history of the church since the time of the apostles could also be written from prison records. Wycliffe, Huss, Savanarola, Calvin, and Tyndale had their faith tested behind prison bars. Luther spent many months of his life under house arrest. Saint John of the Cross wrote his *Spiritual Canticle* from a prison experience. The Worcester jail was the setting for George Fox's *Journal,* and John Bunyan penned *Pilgrim's Progress* during his second imprisonment.

In the modern scene, the prison record changes. There are evangelical Christians who have prison stories that are remarkable. The missionaries in China during the Second World War, the followers of Christ in communist countries, and the victims of religious as well as political persecution — these people will join the honor roll of prisoners for Jesus Christ. But the prominent leaders and the turning points in our spiritual history have faded from the prison record. That is, unless you want to write that history outside the sphere of evangelical Christianity.

What is the significance of the fact that non-evangelicals are the prisoners of the today? Dietrich Bonhoeffer wrote *The Cost of Discipleship* in a Nazi prison, and yet he led the trend toward a religionless Christianity. Cardinal Joseph Mindszenty, a Roman Catholic, would also answer to the roll call of modern prisoners who refuse to compromise their faith. Will Martin Luther King and Ralph Abernathy be written into the prison history of the church? Is our circle of love wide enough to take in the Berrigan brothers who still insist that their civil disobedience is in the will of God?

Even though the recent history of evangelical Christianity cannot be written from a prison record, the early leaders of the revival movement did not forget prisons or the prisoners. One of the results of the Wesleyan Revival in England in the eighteenth century was prison reform. John Wesley considered it a minister's duty to visit prisoners, publicize bad prison conditions, and actively support reform movements. In one of the earliest Methodist conferences in 1788, ministers of the new church were pledged to the duty of visiting those in prison. Out of this climate came John Howard, "The Father of Prison Reform," who openly acknowledged that John Wesley was the inspiration for his work in the councils and Parliament of England. When revivalism came to America in the nineteenth century, a prison ministry came, too. As a result of revival, a United States Christian Commission was formed for ministering to the poor, including those who were in prison. In the twentieth century, however, the prison ministry of evangelical Christians begins to fade. There are examples of jail services and visitation programs, but participation in prison reform has been left to other agencies.

Attica is a reminder that many prisons continue to be the cesspools of society. Despite the efforts at reform, prisons still breed violence, perversion, insanity, and criminality. Penologists talk about "individual treatment" for prisoners. Attempts are made to introduce improved classification systems, wall-less camps, conjugal visits, and inmate councils. Still, custody is custody. Most prison wardens and guards develop the hard-nosed attitude that rehabilitation in prison is a dreamy hope. They get their evidence from the fact that riots can begin in even the most liberal of penal institutions. Individual treatment seems to be no guarantee against violence.

What can evangelical Christians do today for prisons and prisoners? First of all, prison reform has been low on the agenda of legislative action because the public still believes in "cash register justice." In the Old Testament, this was described as the talion principle: "An eye for an eye, and a tooth for a tooth." In practical terms, this means that a prisoner gets what he deserves. He must forfeit his rights as a citizen. He will be segregated from constructive human contacts and must accept whatever dehumanizing effects that a serial number, solitary confinement, starvation diets, and prison brutality may mean. Prison, however, cannot take away the right of a prisoner to think and to feel. That's why he is fair game for an advanced education in either crime or revolution. There are those who believe that Attica was just a skirmish for a forthcoming revolutionary campaign in the society at large. Self-preservation alone should prompt us to support prison reform.

Evangelical Christians have a higher motive for prison reform. Motivated by the biblical imperative, our task is to remind our society that man is created in the image of God. People who have been saved from the condemnation they deserve should be the first to tell the world that God has not given up on mankind. Furthermore, if we hope to preach the gospel to the prisoner, it will more readily be received in a humane climate. Otherwise, the prisoner has the right to ask, "What have you done about my treatment as a man?" It is not too much to expect that national, regional, and local evangelical associations should have a committee on prison ministries. Prospective ministers should be encouraged to consider prison chaplaincies. Information should be circulated on the conditions of prisons, and support should be given to legislation that promotes prison reform.

Individual action can also be taken by concerned Christians. In the State of Washington, there is an "M-2" program in which individual men volunteer to be regular visitors to prisoners who have been rejected by families and friends. The percentage of prison rejects is astounding. Furthermore, the prisoner without outside contacts has the poorest chance for parole and the greatest risk for return. Eighty percent of the rejected men return to prison for breaking parole or being involved in new crimes. The M-2 program turns those statistics around. When these same prisoners become involved in the M-2 program, the rate of recidivism or returns to prison is cut in half. The M-2 program is led by evangelical Christians. It means time, sacrifice, and a risk, but few other areas of lay ministry have such a high return. The program illustrates why the Scriptures are so specific about prisons and prisoners. These are the men who are ready for the gospel as well as for revolution.

Attica has given us another unusual opportunity to demonstrate the love of the Christian and the potency of the gospel. Program similar to "M-2" should become a part of men's fellowships in local churches who are looking for a project. "W-2" programs should be encouraged in women's fellowships and missionary societies. If it's not already too late, we can still put evangelical Christianity back into prison where it belongs.

QUESTIONS

1. Why did Jesus emphasize visiting those in prison as a test question at the final judgment (Matt. 25)? Do you think that we will have to answer it literally? How will you answer?

2. On what basis should Christians be ready to go to prison? Is civil disobedience limited to obeying God and preaching the Gospel, or does it include protesting injustice and inhumanity which might lead to arrest? For what moral issue would you be willing to go to jail?

3. According to predictions, hostility toward evangelical Christians will increase as secularism and pluralism become dominant in our society. With 60 percent of the Christians in the world already under persecution, do you foresee Christians in America jailed for their faith sometime in the future? If so, what do you think the specific charge will be?

4. Prisons are schools for crime. Criminologists recommend that young and first-time convicts be separated from seasoned criminals. What part should Christians play in the legislation for prison reform to prevent the repetition of crime as well as to encourage rehabilitation of the prisoners?

5. Forgotten people in prison leave behind wives, children, and families in shame. How can the church minister to the particular needs of these people?

9

How Do You Tell
a Poor Man
that God Loves Him?

A revolution that began two hundred years ago is still unfinished. In the last third of the eighteenth century, the revolution centered in the demand for *political* equality. That revolution continues today with the demands of minorities for political power and individual rights. But before this revolution was finished, the last third of the nineteenth century saw the wheel of revolution turn toward *social* equality. It was the natural counterpart of the revolution for political equality, and it continues today in the demands for the elimination of social barriers that have been erected by race, creed, sex, age, education, and wealth.

It should be no surprise that another turn of the revolutionary wheel in the last third of the twentieth century should raise the cry of the poor for *economic* equality. The demands for the reduction of political, social, and economic differences are part and parcel of the same powerful human drive for equality. Therefore, when the black and the poor press their claim for a share of the wealth, it is not simply the question of a conspiracy against the system; it is evidence of the continuing revolution that began with the shot that was heard around the world two hundred years ago.

If the pattern of the revolutions for political and social equality is repeated in the struggle for economic equality, it is just a matter of time before there will be large-scale breakthroughs on the problems of poverty. Minimum wage standards, the graduated income tax, and the welfare programs have served as introductions to the revolution for economic equality. A guaranteed annual income is the next turn of the revolutionary wheel. The fact that the principle of a guaranteed income has now been supported by both political parties is sufficient evidence to predict that such a program will be enacted as law in a year or two. Support from the conservative Christian community for these programs, however, will not come until the ethical and theological barriers which have been erected against the redistribution of wealth have been broken down.

Similar ethical and theological problems were encountered in the previous revolutions. From the distance of two hundred years, the eighteenth-century revolution for political equality is seen as the legitimate expression of Christian values in the American democratic system. At the time, however, the advocates of political equality were enemies of an orthodoxy of authority as it was specified in the doctrine of the "divine right of kings." Even the perspective of one hundred years makes a difference. The nineteenth-century revolution for social equality is now remembered as the natural response to Christianity's emphasis upon individual worth. The struggle of the time, however, had to be waged against an orthodoxy of election as it was specified in the doctrine of the "chosen people." Although both of these revolutions are far advanced, the orthodoxies of authority and election are still invoked when a turn of the revolutionary wheel threatens culturalized Christianity.

The twentieth-century revolution for economic equality

is also more than a conflict between the rich and the poor; it is heavily weighted with ethical and theological overtones. For instance, Christians have a difficult time reconciling the redistribution of wealth because they have taken literally Christ's words, "Ye have the poor with you always" (Mark 14:7). When this statement is generalized out of context, it becomes a social theology that supports the belief that poverty is inevitable. Extended to its logical extreme, the belief also sanctifies an economic caste system that is just as fatalistic as the secular doctrine of social determinism. It also provides an escape hatch for the Christian who needs to justify his lack of involvement in the poverty question.

Closely related to this pessimism about the poor is the belief that poverty is the result of sin. The words of the psalmist are quoted as a proof text for this position, "Yet have I not seen the righteous forsaken, nor his seed begging bread" (Psalm 37:25). More than this, there is the promise that the righteous shall prosper. Since Jesus said, "Seek ye first the kingdom of God, and his righteousness; and all these things shall be added unto you" (Matthew 6:33), His words are interpreted as a divine sanction for material success. Put against the current concern for the poor, the spiritualized doctrine of poverty reads like a two-sided coin — one side has the inscription, "It is a sin to be poor"; the other side has the motto, "It is righteous to be rich."

This doctrine of poverty is closer to the Protestant Ethic than it is to biblical truth. Material prosperity was never a guarantee of Christ's message. The confusion between "abundance" and "affluence" is clearly an adaptation for the twentieth century. Yet, this is the orthodoxy that is being challenged by the revolution for economic equality which began when Michael Harrington identified the "culture of poverty."

If Christians are saying, "It is a sin to be poor," the defendants of the poor are saying, "It is a sin to allow a man to be poor." Poverty, according to them, is still a sin. The difference is in the identification of the sinner. Their proof text would be the words of James, "If a brother or sister be naked, and destitute of daily food, and one of you say unto them, Depart in peace, be ye warmed and filled; notwithstanding ye give them not those things which are needful to the body; what doth it profit" (James 2:15-16)? Then, they have the statistics of affluence to back them up. The latest official economic projections show a gross national product for the United States that will rise to three trillion dollars within the century. This means that our post-industrial society will become more affluent and that we will have the economic resources to do whatever we will to do — including the elimination of poverty.

The advocates of economic equality also show the qualitative differences that exist between the "haves" and the "have nots." Not only are there significant discrepancies in personal income and earning power; there are depressing differences in the opportunities for food, clothing, shelter, education, health, and even life itself. Evidently, the poverty of life is related to the poverty of spirit. Therefore, it is not just a question of personal income, it is a question about the quality of life.

When Arthur Fletcher, former Assistant Secretary for Wage and Labor Standards, spoke to this issue, he used the story of the rich young ruler as his case in point. With evangelistic fervor, he recounted the story of the rich man's righteousness. But he said that the acid test of that man's qualification for eternal life was his willingness to give his wealth to the poor. Mr. Fletcher was not advocating an arbitrary give-away program to the poor. Rather, he was calling Christians to rise up as constituency for social justice in job opportunities. His warning was that the creation of jobs by which the wealth might be shared was the alternative to the frustration among the poor that will eventually lead to violence. He was not posing an idle threat. As the nation becomes more wealthy, economists have already predicted that the gap between the rich and poor will continue to widen unless there is direct intervention by national policy. Without such a policy, James Reston has warned us, there is the possibility that the powerless poor will take their case to the streets as the blacks have already done.

What should be the Christian response to the revolution for economic equality?

First, Christians will have to look critically at the connections that have been made between their theological position and their cultural heritage. The Protestant Ethic which equates hard work with financial success as evidence of the favor of God provides incentive for individual action, but it severely limits social programs for the alleviation of poverty. The ''sweat of the brow'' philosophy behind the Protestant Ethic is not adequate to encompass the majority of workers who today are in service professions which rely on brains and heart rather than brawn. Also, financial success has become a declining quality among youth who are placing human values ahead of vocational achievement. In the future, these concepts will undergo even more radical change as automation replaces the arm of man and the computer takes over many of his basic intellectual functions. In tomorrow's ethic of work centers in intellectual, managerial, and service professions, some major adjustments will have to be made in our thinking about our responsibility for those who lack the potential for these tasks. This is the reason why Christians should not get their theology locked into an ethic with cultural roots that can be undercut by social change. Yet, the protection that the Protestant Ethic gave to the dignity of man needs to be retained when there is a tendency to respond to mass needs with mass methods that hide abuses and corrupt the individual.

Second, Christians will have to search diligently in the Scriptures for a biblical perspective on poverty. Is poverty inevitable? Because poverty is an attitude as well as a situation, it appears as if relative poverty will always be with us. But it is immoral to use the Scriptures as a basis for Christians' refusing to work to raise the economic level of every person in an affluent nation above the point of starvation and hopelessness.

Is it a sin to be poor? Christians tussled with the same question earlier in the century when medical break-throughs prompted the question, "Is it a sin to be sick?" The same answer seems to apply in both cases. Sickness and poverty can be the result of sin, but this should not deter us from doing everything possible to treat the problems and eliminate the conditions out of which the problems are bred. At the same time, Christians must resist the opposite temptation that equates the alleviation of poverty with redemption. Christians must be involved in the revolution for economic equality, not only because they are concerned citizens, but also because the man who is freed from the poverty of life should be ready to respond to questions about the poverty of the spirit.

Third, Christians will have to establish a priority for

their own personal values. At the national level, the priority question is created by the evidence that the rising gross national product will make it possible to alleviate the conditions of poverty if we choose. As the nonviolent black protesters have illustrated, the twenty-four billion dollars that was spent to put a man on the moon could also have tipped the scale in the relief of the poor during the same decade, if poverty had been the national priority.

A similar value conflict is created with the question, "Is it a sin to allow a man to be poor?" in an affluent society. This drives the issue directly to the pocketbook of the comfortable Christian. It may mean a vote for taxes. It may mean hiring an unskilled worker who must be trained. It may mean a vote for a welfare system that feeds hungry children while it protects a negligent mother. It may mean leadership for a church program to adopt poverty families. It may also mean support of a guaranteed income for displaced and unemployed workers that will include some professional freeloaders. It does not mean that abuses are overlooked, but it may require a priority decision between the sin of the poor and the sin of the affluent.

Actually, Christians should be leaders in the war on poverty. They have the motive of Christ who made the poor His people. They have the cultural ethic which protects against give-away programs that destroy human initiative. They have the biblical perspective for sharing their wealth with a brother in need. As John Bennett has said, "There is a revolutionary bias in Christianity in favor of the poor." Yet, this bias has been overlooked because we have assumed that poverty is inevitable and that the poor deserve their lot. Today, those conditions have been changed so that we are without excuse. Our nation now has the wealth to relieve the poor, but the moral responsibility rests with those who hold the economic power. We also know that if our Christian compassion does not cause us to rise to meet our brother's need, the poor will have the power to drive us up against the wall. Therefore, whether out of compassion or fear, we need to reread, repent, and respond to John's words, "But as for the well-to-do man who sees his brother in want but shuts his eyes — and his heart — how could anyone believe that the love of God lives in him" (I John 3:17 Phillips)?

For concerned Christians, the answer is rhetorical.

QUESTIONS

1. "Seek ye first the kingdom of God and his righteousness; and all these things will be added unto you" (Matt. 6:33) is often quoted to justify affluence as evidence of the blessing of God. Is this what Jesus meant? If not, what lesson was He teaching?

2. When the Gentile Christians took up a collection for starving Jewish Christians in Jerusalem, each one gave "according to his ability" (Acts 11:29). Does this action suggest a graduated tithe for Christians in an affluent society to assist needy Christians at home and abroad? How would you implement such a proposal?

3. Jesus met several wealthy people. Did He deal with them according to a single principle or individually? What lessons can we learn from His experience as our response to wealth today?

4. When Jesus said, "For ye have the poor always with you . . ." (Matt. 26:11), did He mean that poverty is inevitable? If yes, why give to the poor if the problem can never be solved? If no, what did Jesus mean and how does it affect our attitude toward poverty?

5. Capitalists argue that economic growth through free enterprise will attack poverty by raising the standard of living for everyone. Socialists counter by saying that economic equality will be gained only by state planning and control of wealth. Why is capitalism

and free enterprise considered most compatible with Christianity? Can the church lead the capitalistic system into greater social responsibility without increasing the power of the state?

10

Is This
the Woman's ERA?

She was introduced to me as the Chairman of the Women's Liberation Movement. I tried to charm her by walking through the door ahead of her and refusing to stand or pull out her chair when she sat down beside me at lunch. Still the conversation started with a confrontation. She asked, "Do you realize that the Declaration of Independence begins with the words, 'All *men* are created equal' "?

I answered, "No, I've never thought of it that way."

Her retort was, "That's just the trouble. You've never thought of it that way — and that makes you a *sexist!*"

After having my curiosity quickened by that accusation, I decided to learn more about the Women's Liberation Movement. Before this encounter with one of the leaders, I had assumed that I could support Representative Martha Griffith's drive for a constitutional amendment to end sexual discrimination while laughing off the "Burn the Bra" demonstrations of extremists. Now, with the danger of a little knowledge, I find that I am a Male Chauvinist of the lowest order. As a Man, an Administrator, a Husband, and a Christian, everything that I say or do can be interpreted as an indication of my oppressive, discriminating, exploiting, and patriarchal attitude toward women. With that admission, I can only ask for a fair hearing of my bias.

The Women's Liberation Movement is too splintered to sum up its cause with the single word "equality." Fem

Lib groups range from women establishmentarians who want equal rights, jobs, and wages to female revolutionaries who want to destroy capitalism by freeing women from sex, marriage, and the family. Because equality means so many things, it is important to know the differences.

Legal Equality for Women. The House of Representatives has passed an amendment to the Constitution of the United States that reads, "Equality of rights under the law shall not be denied or abridged by the United States or any state on account of sex." The vote on the amendment was 350 to 16. It will still require the approval of the Senate and three-fourths of the state legislatures before it becomes law. If ratified, more than one thousand state laws which discriminate against women would be invalidated. Such laws include "community property" laws which designate the husband as the head of the household and do not permit the wife to obtain a credit rating against the jointly-held property. There are also divorce laws which make adultery a woman's problem and a man's case. Opponents of the amendment, however, point out that the laws which protect women would also be dropped. Women could be drafted for military service, required to work longer hours, hired to lift heavy weights, and assigned to any hazardous job. The traditional legal demands on the "head of the household" could be reversed. In divorce suits, a man might be favored to gain custody of the children, and a woman might be required to pay alimony to her former husband.

Economic Equality for Women. The case for job discrimination against women is clear. On the national average, working women receive one-half as much as working men. Their salaries are lower even when the job and the educational requirements are the same. They are seldom found in the high-ranking positions of business, government, or education. As the Fem Lib literature describes the economic position of women, "They are hired last, fired first, paid less, passed over for promotion, and bored with routine jobs." The women's argument has taken on additional strength with a recently published Chase Manhattan Bank Report which shows that the economic gap between men and women in the world of work is becoming wider each year.

The drive for economic equality has been carried by the National Organization for Women (NOW). In a Bill of Rights for Women, they have asked for equal employment, maternity leaves, tax deductions for child care, day care centers, and job-training opportunities. Cold cash is a major motive in the liberation of women.

Social Equality for Women. The demands for economic equality are directly tied to the social roles into which women are cast by the culture in which we live. Even though 51 percent of the population is female, a male-dominated culture has made them a minority group. Miss Elinor Kaine, the first woman to announce a professional football game, has said,

> All men and women can pause to rethink the question, "What is a woman?" If the answer is helpmate, baby-maker, pleasure toy, madonna, cook, or secretary, as many of us think it is, then we should rethink further. Those are prejudices, not answers. Perhaps we can begin with the ultra-radical notion that a woman is a human being.

This statement strikes a common chord with all minority movements. Blacks, students, and women contend that they are made less than human when they

91

are forced into separate and subordinate roles. With the women's liberationists, the sting is in the idea that women are the "weaker sex." The corollary is that they are the oppressed and exploited objects of the "stronger sex." Even Tennyson becomes a male chauvinist because he wrote,

> Man for the field and woman for the hearth;
> Man for the sword and for the needle she;
> Man with the head and woman with the heart;
> Man to command and woman to obey;
> All else confusion.

Confusion does exist. The implications of merging male and female roles range from amusing to devastating. Although there is very little humor in revolutionary movements, one speaker for Fem Lib did a take-off on an old saw when she said, "If God had wanted women to stay in the kitchen, He would have given them aluminum hands." A Catholic woman writer followed through with true humor when she announced, "We shall witness the complete removal of discrimination in the Catholic Church on the day when there is a pregnant pope who is either African or Asiatic." The humor disappears, however, when radical women of the New Left get into the act. They maintain that the capitalistic society has used sexual discrimination as a device to exploit women. Therefore, they not only oppose legal and economic discrimination, but also marriage and the family. Marriage, to them, is a form of "legalized rape" which supports an outmoded patriarchal society. In that same society, the family is a tool to keep the woman in her place. For these extremists, the liberation of woman is a revolutionary cause which will be accomplished only when the institutions of Western culture have been pulled up by their roots and destroyed.

Sexual Equality for Women. The biological differences between men and women are a part of the contest for women's rights. While the differences are too obvious to evoke serious debate, there are direct moves to narrow the gap between sexes. "Burn the Bra" demonstrations and marches at the Miss America contests are in revolt against women as ornaments for the visual pleasures of men. "Unisexual dress" patterns are designed to reduce the physical differences between sexes. The double standard of sexual behavior is also in question. Society has tended to forgive the unvirtuous man, but never the unvirtuous woman. The Pill was supposed to have freed women from the consequences of pregnancy in premarital or extramarital sex. Women of the liberation, however, believe that The Pill has only made women more available for dominating men.

Because sexual differences cannot be denied, the argument enters the psychological arena when Women's Liberationists contend that there are no differences in temperament or personality between men and women. Tennyson's suggestion that man has the "head" and woman has the "heart" is condemned as discrimination. Freud's theory of the Oedipus complex in which a girl competes with her mother for the father's love is considered prejudicial psychology. Erickson's view that a man has the strength of "outer space" and women have the power of "inner space" is equally discriminatory. Even the evidence that men are physically stronger and more competitive is rejected as culturally determined.

The demand for sexual equality has its revolutionary extremes. In the revolutionary organizations of SNCC and the SDS, women joined under the assumption that they would be equals with men. /The dream was shattered, however, when Stokely Carmichael said: "The position of women in this movement is prone." The same has been true of the SDS and the Weathermen so that the women have split off into their own revolutionary movement. Their revolt is not only against marriage and the family; they are rejecting heterosexual relationships and the reproductive role of women. The literature suggests that sexual equality for women will be gained by homosexual relationships, women's communes, and (just in case) liberalized abortion laws.

Women's liberation cannot be dismissed as ridiculous, revolutionary, unscientific, and unchristian. /There are elements in the case that deserve serious consideration. There are other phases of the movement that need to be known and resisted. Our responsibility is to know the differences between the two. As Christians, the testing begins with the Word of God. Immediately, a majority of the Fem Lib will call "foul" because they view the Bible as a sexist book. The notable omission in the Women's Liberation Movement, however, is the absence of the question about the *spiritual equality* of women. Therefore, to give the case a full and fair hearing, it is worthwhile to know how the Bible speaks to the issue.

The first biblical principle for womanhood is her creation in the image of God. Genesis 1:27 leaves no doubt about her *spiritual equality* with man, "So God created man in his own image, in the image of God created he him; male and female created he them." Even though God created woman out of man, she was spiritually one with man in both her personhood and in her potential. Women's Lib contends strongly for woman as a person, but vaguely as to her origin. There is no question in the

Word of God. A man and a woman are equal as persons created in the image of God. Spiritually, personhood is more important than womanhood.

A second biblical principle relates to the biological differences and the personal relationships between a man and a woman. "And the Lord God said, It is not good that the man should be alone; I will make him a help meet for him" (Genesis 2:18). "And Adam said, This is now bone of my bones, and flesh of my flesh: she shall be called Woman, because she was taken out of Man. Therefore shall a man leave his father and his mother, and shall cleave unto his wife: and they shall be one flesh" (Genesis 2:23-25). This scripture establishes the complementary relationship between a man and a woman. It states that a man needs a woman psychologically, functionally, and physically. A woman complements a man because of her differences. It is unrealistic to deny that those differences exist. The distinction of womanhood is next only to the equality of her personhood. Therefore, if the complementary relationship between a man and a woman who are physically, psychologically, and functionally different is prejudice, the Bible will have to stand as a sexist document. All the evidence, however, is on the side of differences that are biologically inherited and beautifully complemented in marriage when man and woman become "one flesh."

The third biblical principle is least acceptable to the Women's Liberation Movement. As a result of sin (both a compliment and a condemnation to a woman's curiosity), the functional roles of men and women were separated. The woman was to bear her children with sorrow and the man was to rule over her. The man, in turn, was to learn the difference between good and evil with sorrow and to earn a living by the sweat of his brow. The Edenic principles of personhood and womanhood were shattered by sin and, therefore, had to be determined by law. The tragic error of both reformers and revolutionaries is the assumption that personhood and womanhood can be recovered by freedom from the law but without the freedom of grace.

Jesus Christ restored personhood and womanhood to its spiritual perspective. Legal discrimination against a woman made stoning her the punishment for adultery. In a case history, however, Jesus declared the equality of men and women before the law when He said, "He that is without sin among you, let him first cast a stone at her" (John 8:7). More important, the primacy of personhood was illustrated as He said to the guilty woman, "Go, and sin no more" (John 8:11). If this case can be used as an example, Jesus would apply the same principles of personhood and equality in the legal and economic issues for women in today's post-industrial society.

There are biblical references which suggest discrimination against women. Paul is the worst offender as he argues for plain, silent, and submissive women because God created man first and a woman sinned first. (I Timothy 2:9-15.) That argument is exclusively Paul's, but his purpose is shared by Peter who said that women should be adorned in "a meek and quiet spirit." (I Peter 3:4.) Peter also expressed the consistent biblical view that women were "weaker vessels" (I Peter 3:7) and subject to their husbands. This position, however, does not stand alone as male dominance. In the same context, husbands are called upon to love their wives as "Christ also loved the church, and gave himself for it" (Ephesians 5:25). In this complementary relationship, the spiritual equality of men and women comes forward again as Peter states the ultimate goal of becoming "heirs together of the grace of life" (I Peter 3:7).

Women's liberationists who protest the complementary relationship of men and women in marriage should also remember the women who were honored for achievements other than being obedient wives or faithful mothers. Deborah was a judge who complemented Barak's brawn with her brains; Esther was an aggressive advocate for her people; and Miriam was a prophetess. Even the male chauvinist, Paul, recognized the businesswoman, Lydia; the co-minister, Priscilla; and the missionary servant, Phoebe. All biblical women outside the home are not the Delilahs and the Jezebels that male sexists and female liberationists would have us believe. There is more freedom within the biblical view than outside of it.

How do we respond to women's liberation? The attitude of Jesus Christ is our guide. Woman, as a person created in the image of God, is more important than biological differences, social roles, economic status, or legal rights. This does not, however, deny the complementary roles of the sexes which are fulfilled in marriage and the home. The personhood of the woman and the womanhood of the person should then be protected by equal rights before the law and in economic opportunity. Christians should oppose legal or defacto discrimination against the personhood of women at the same time that they contend for laws and social standards that maintain womanhood, the home, and the family. Educational and economic equality should be guaranteed for women who may not desire to marry. But, when women's liberation reaches out to deny the differences between sexes, to prevent heterosexual relations, and to seek to destroy marriage and the family, it should be exposed and resisted by Christian activists. We cannot accept Gloria Steinem's sarcastic tirade which peaks with the shout, "A woman needs a man like a fish needs a bicycle."

But, on the other hand, have you ever met a pregnant bishop?

QUESTIONS

1. Women's liberation, which began with the Equal Rights Amendment, mushroomed into a moral issue with fundamentalists on one extreme and lesbians on the other. How can a Christian discriminate among the issues and take a position without being forced into one camp or the other?

2. Is there reconciliation between Paul's words "Let the woman learn in silence with all subjection" (I Tim. 2:11) and his commendation of Priscilla as a helper in Christ Jesus who, with her husband, instructed Apollos in the way of God (Acts 18:26)?

3. Proponents of equality for women downplay or deny physical differences between the sexes. Genesis 2 explicitly divides the sexes and implies different, but complementary, roles and relationships based upon sex. Using Genesis 2 as a reference, what do human beings have in common as persons and what do men and women have as unique complements of their sex?

4. Ordination of women is a controversy which splits denominations and congregations. What is the theological argument against the ordination of women in the Roman Catholic and Episcopal Churches? Why is it not a controversy in most of the non-liturgical denominations and evangelical churches? Is there a Biblical perspective on this issue?

5. Strange as it seems, local churches are sustained by women and controlled by men. Why? What changes would you anticipate in the social structure and the ministry of the church if women came into co-leadership?

11

What Do You Do
When the Pump Runs Dry?

Americans have joined the wretched of the earth. A few months ago, poor and hungry people were faceless foreigners to whom we sent CARE packages. Now, with poetic justice, the balloon of our affluence has been pricked by shortages of crisis proportions. In rapid succession, beef, toilet tissue, and gasoline have all come up short. While none of these items is absolutely essential to our survival, we do need them to sustain our well-fed, refined, and mobile civilization. Driven from indulgence to necessity, we are now neighbors with the "have-nots."

Shortages are predicted to come and go for the rest of our lives. In the past, we have been so preoccupied with our growth that we have scorned the prophets who foresaw the end of plenty. Twenty-seven years ago, for instance, a study of natural resources predicted the energy crisis. No one paid heed to the need to conserve our fuel resources. Consequently, we are faced with shortages that are not just politically contrived by Arabs and economically contrived by the oil industry. A team of scientists on our campus recently concluded that the pervasive questions for the rest of this century will be energy-related. Through the 1970s, the man on the street will be asked to save fuel and the man in the laboratory will be asked to develop new sources of energy from the sun, wind, water, sand, and even from garbage. Then, in the 1980s, the issue will turn to the implications of our energy policies upon personal and social behavior. We have already seen the effect of moderate shortages upon our style of life. Our mobility has been curtailed by the fuel crisis and our eating habits have been changed because of the price of meat. Greater implications are yet ahead. Bridging over into the 1990s will be the ethical questions about our energy policies. For example, "Project Independence" called for national self-sufficiency in energy by 1980. While the goal may be scientifically feasible, is it morally right? At the same time that we are becoming a "global village" in communications and "space earth" in the environment, can we become "isolationists" in energy?

Social and moral questions arising from shortages will come even closer to our homes if food also becomes scarce. Talk of world famine has circulated for some time. The seers have usually been written off as Bible-thumpers or crystal gazers, but now the prophets include research scientists who come armed with facts and humility. By the 1980s, they predict, we will have food shortages that will send us to bed either hungry or broke. Yet, consistent with our complacency, we will wait for the crisis before we act. Then, citizens will fight on bread lines, politicians will use hunger to get votes, and scientists will get emergency funding to develop new food sources, such as fish meal from the sea.

How do Christians live with shortages? Jesus anticipated this question in His Sermon on the Mount. His hearers were poor people who did not have enough to eat, drink, or wear. To them, he gave some principles that are flashing a new meaning for shortage-conscious Christians.

When Jesus talked about shortages, He referred to *needs* rather than *wants*. Food, water, clothing, and shelter are *needs;* culture, wealth, and status are *wants*.

Because affluence frees us from needs, most of us have been exclusively concerned with wants. Jesus, however, spoke only of needs when He set down the principle: "Do not be anxious about your life, what you shall eat or what you shall drink, nor about your body, what you shall put on. Is not life more than food, and the body more than clothing" (Matthew 6:25, RSV)? With this principle, He coupled the promise: "Look at the birds of the air: they neither sow nor reap nor gather into barns, and yet your heavenly Father feeds them. Are you not of more value than they" (Matthew 6:26, RSV)?

His *principle* is that life and health are more important than food and clothing, and His *promise* is that God will meet our needs because of the value He has placed upon us. So far, we have had only limited experience in applying the principle or believing the promise. If shortages continue and become more severe, however, we may find ourselves anxious about our needs rather than our wants.

Christ's sermon also stressed the need to trust in God rather than in yourself (or the government, which is an extension of yourself) when there are shortages. Unmet needs bring out the selfishness and the submissiveness in man. Selfishness, as a primitive instinct for survival, has been displayed in fights that have broken out at gasoline stations when someone tried to crash the line. For those who would rather submit than fight, there is the tendency to trust in the government to set up a rationing system that will equalize the shortage.

Jesus did not advocate trust in either yourself or the State. He taught that Christians will trust God to supply their needs. Radical though it may sound, Jesus said, "Your heavenly Father knows that you need . . . all these things. . ." (Matthew 6:32, RSV). I talked about this principle of trust in a sermon last week. My hypothetical case was a man who had to commute one hundred miles a day to work. I said that he may have to trust God for the solution if the government limits his gas to forty-five gallons a month. After the service, a man met me at the door and said, "I'm the guy and I've been worried sick about it." My answer was, "In order to fulfill His promise to meet our basic needs, God has to have our basic trust." Then I remembered that I commute only one block to work (and usually drive). I had the theory, but he had the problem.

Shortages test our mental health as well as our trust. Jesus used the word "anxiety" to describe the personal crisis of people without adequate food, water, and clothing. Psychiatrists speak of "anxiety" when a patient is obsessed by a fear that destroys his effectiveness as a person. In contrast, "worry" is a legitimate concern in proper proportion to the problem. A Christian father may "worry" about food for his children in the future, but he need not be so "anxious" that he loses his effectiveness as a parent.

Jesus said, "Why be anxious?" Then He answered His question with other questions, "Doesn't God care?" and "What difference will it make?" To a person who is already anxiety-ridden, these questions may seem brutal, but Jesus wasn't being sarcastic. Rather than just saying "Cool it," He said, "Use the same energy to seek the kingdom of God, and God will take care of your needs." Sometime in the future, when our needs are short, we will have to relearn that lesson.

Time marches backward in a shortage. Poor and hungry people do not live greedily for the future. The sum and substance of their existence is today's need and the dread of tomorrow's lack. A faint semblance of this time perspective came to me the other night when I was told in station after station that there was no gas. I had to stop short of my destination and take a motel room. My last thought before I dropped off to a fatigued sleep was, "But what if there is no gas tomorrow?" In answer to my question, Jesus said, "Do not be anxious about tomorrow, for tomorrow will be anxious for itself. Let the day's own trouble be sufficient for the day" (Matthew 6:34, RSV).

Jesus' sermon on shortages culminates in the principle that our witness gains meaning in a time of need. Life-styles are changed by shortages. When the fifty-five miles per hour speed limit was imposed in our state, a husband and wife arrived late for a meeting at Seattle Pacific College. Rather than apologize, the husband said, "You know, at fifty-five, I saw things along the freeway that I had missed at seventy. His wife added, "Yes, and this was the first chance that we've had to talk in a long time."

Cadillacs are replaced by Pintos, oil tanks are replaced by windmills, and tenderloin steak is replaced by Hamburger Helper! What a time for a Christian witness! We can huddle with a spoiled generation of Americans and backpedal with a groan, or we can stretch out with the witness of simple trust and a simple life. Even skeptics would listen to the gospel according to affluent Christians who set their standard of living at the level of basic needs and gave the difference to the poor. Their witness would be consistent with Jesus' preaching when He said, "Do not lay up for yourselves treasures on earth, ... but lay up for yourselves treasures in heaven" (Matthew 6:19, 20, RSV). Was He saying that earth is for *needs* and heaven is for *wants?* If so, we may be investing in the wrong world. In the meantime, we can also heed Henry David Thoreau's words of human wisdom, "A man is rich who makes his wants few."

A Christian witness comes in many forms, but the most effective always cuts across the grain of the times. Love in the midst of hate; peace in turmoil; and joy in sorrow. Simplicity is the key. In the midst of shortages, simple needs, simple trust, and a simple life will fill our horn of plenty.

QUESTIONS

1. Even with Alaskan oil, America is predicted to run out of petroleum resources within ten years. Adequate new energy sources cannot be developed within this period of time and the nation will not have the money to buy foreign oil. If this happens, what will be the effect on the balance of power and international relations? Is crisis, catastrophe, or war inevitable? What would be the effect upon us to lose our position as a dominant super-power?

2. The stewardship of resources is a Biblical concept that is being rediscovered by secular environmentalists without acknowledging its roots in revelation. Using Genesis 1-2 as your reference, what truths about the nature of God, man, and the earth give foundation to our stewardship responsibilities?

3. Energy shortages are predicted to alter the lifestyle of Americans. What changes in travel, food, clothing, and shelter would you foresee if we run out of oil and do not have adequate energy alternatives? How would the ministry of the church be affected?

4. Some churches are proposing Christian condominiums centered around extended family relationships, home worship, and cooperative buying. What are the advantages and disadvantages of such plans for the mission of the church and Christians in the world?

5. Through the ages, Christian witness has been accompanied by personal discipline in the stewardship of time, money, talent, and natural resources. What personal disciplines could churches introduce today which would enhance a Christian witness in the world?

12

Why Do We Make Play
Such Hard Work?

Almost one hundred years ago, President James A. Garfield said that the history of the human race can be divided into two chapters. Chapter 1 is the fight to get leisure; Chapter 2 is what to do with it after you get it.

Garfield's prediction has come true. After two centuries of striving for the fulfillment of the American dream under the ideal of the work ethic, leisure has been won. The only problem is that we do not know what to do with it.

Leisure in the twentieth century is a new experience in the history of man. Never before has leisure been the opportunity of the masses rather than the classes. Ancient civilizations that were built upon a slave economy had leisure classes. Today, however, science and technology have made it possible for more people to work less time for more money. The result is an affluence of time in which the masses can choose activities that are not strictly for either existence or subsistence. Time has become a luxury as the masses of people work shorter days, shorter weeks, and shorter careers. In fact, a study has shown that the amount of time that executives work during the week is increasing at the same time that the work week for their employees is decreasing. This has led someone to remark that the social scale for work and leisure has been totally tipped. At one time we had the leisure classes and the working masses, but now we are moving toward the working classes and the leisure masses!

Too little attention has been given to the social and moral implications of a leisure society. Unsuspectingly, the central motive for our life is changing. Rather than organizing our life around work, leisure becomes the center for our planning. A generation ago, we worked in order to enjoy leisure. Today, the question is whether we use leisure in order to enjoy work. Socially and morally, we have not begun to face this issue. Yet, we would concur with the opinion that the tone of a society is determined by the quality of its leisure.

Christianity has been caught off guard by the reversing roles of leisure and work. In the creation story, God worked for six days and then rested. When Adam and Eve were expelled from Eden, part of their punishment was to work by the "sweat of their brow." Sin had an effect upon the joy of work as well as the nature of rest. Therefore, when the commandments were given, a Sabbath day was set aside from work for the purpose of rest and worship. Because the Sabbath time was so precisely defined, it was not leisure. Rest was prescribed in order that the worker, his animals, his family, and strangers ". . . may be refreshed" (Exodus 23:12) to work again. Leisure is better defined as optional time in which a person can make his own choices for self-fulfillment after his obligations are met.

Biblical history was written in an age when the demands for existence and subsistence dominated a person's time. It is not surprising that the writer of the Proverbs extolled the wisdom of work and the folly of the idle. This same theme was carried through in the New Testament when sloth was listed as one of the seven deadly sins and Christians were admonished not to be "slothful in business" in the same breath in which they were called to be "fervent in spirit; serving the Lord" (Romans 12:11).

Idleness was not the only evil against which Christians were warned. There seems to be connection between ease and riches. Jesus himself told the parable of the rich man who was a fool because he reached the point of affluence when he could say, "Soul, take thine ease. . . ." To Jesus, time as well as money is a resource for which a man is responsible.

Greek thought also influenced the view of work and leisure among early Christians. In Hebrews, there is a Platonic touch as flesh becomes identified with evil and the spirit with good. Emphasis is also given to "rest" as the goal of the Christian. By inference, the author seems to hold a "work now — rest later" philosophy, with work as a form of suffering in the flesh and rest as the reward for a life in the spirit. Augustine followed this same line of thought as he put Christian activities on a scale with contemplation as the highest good. Whether right or wrong, these were the attitudes that produced the artificial distinction between the sacred and the secular that prevailed until the Reformation.

Luther gave work new meaning when he told the converted shoemaker, "It is more spiritual for you to use good leather and a firm last than to pass out tracts." Leisure, however, was still limited to the rich and the royal. Work had been liberated from the realm of evil and suffering, but it had not been given the virtue of an intrinsic good. It took the Industrial Revolution and American capitalism to accomplish that. In order to sanctify the reality of long and hard labor, work was given its own reward as a spiritual value with the promise of God's blessing in prosperity. A complementary doctrine was the evil, not only of idleness, but also of play. Puritanism equated pleasure with sin.

Now that Christians, particularly those of a conservative persuasion, have earned their leisure through hard work, they do not know what to do with it. Old attitudes still prevail. Work is good and idleness is evil, but leisure is a new option which is not covered by past doctrines. Furthermore, play is still suspect. As David Reisman has noted, our philosophy of "strenuous work" requires "strenuous leisure." Christians know how to work and how to worship, but they do not know how to play. Consequently, they become easy victims for busy action in their spare time which is neither restful nor recreative. Or, they become part of the idle masses whose spare time can be manipulated by the media, advertising, and social pressure. While guarding against the encroachments of secularism in other areas, the misuse of leisure may be a subtle way in which Christians are squeezed into the world's mold.

A biblical ethic for leisure is difficult to define. Christians will have to be guided by principles rather than by regulations.

First, we will have to accept the fact that our lives will be organized around leisure rather than work.

Second, the non-biblical idea that work is good and leisure is evil will have to be discarded.

Third, the guilt that has condemned pleasure and play will have to be lifted.

Fourth, leisure will have to be recognized as a moral option in which a person can either find or destroy the meaning of life.

Fifth, leisure will have to be considered a new resource

for Christians which is subject to the principles of biblical stewardship.

Sixth, the meaning of leisure as the optional time for self-fulfillment, in contrast to work, rest and worship, will have to be communicated as a potential source of significant living.

Seventh, leisure opportunities will have to be defined as a new freedom which permits a Christian to *rest* from activities, *recreate* himself by the full exercise of his personal gifts beyond *work*, and *extend* himself into new and creative dimensions of his personality.

Eighth, Christians will have to be encouraged to learn to play again without the feeling of guilt from the spontaneity and the pleasure of recreation.

Ninth, because the quality of leisure is related to the quality of work and worship, a rhythm of work, worship, and play will have to be developed by Christians and their churches.

Tenth, if the tone of the society is determined by the quality of its leisure, Christians should have a new area for leadership and witness in which the church can lead the way by helping people learn to use their leisure rightly.

Jesus said, "Consider the lilies of the field, . . . they toil not, neither do they spin: And yet I say unto you, That even Solomon in all his glory was not arrayed like one of these" (Matthew 6:28-29). Bertrand Russell used these words as support for his essay *In Praise of Idleness.* This is a perversion of the Word of God, because idleness is condemned as neither work, rest, nor worship. Jesus, however, may have foreseen the coming of an affluent age which needed a leisure ethic. If so, He may have been praising leisure as a time when the beauty of life can be created and recreated in order to make both our work and our worship equally beautiful.

QUESTIONS

1. According to the Bureau of the Census, Americans have more leisure time and use almost half of it watching television. If you logged a week of your time, approximately what percentage is given to work, rest, worship, and leisure?

2. Is there a common Biblical principle to guide a Christian's approach to work, rest, worship, and leisure? If so, what is it?

3. What is the difference between "ease," "idleness," and "sloth" which are condemned in the Bible and "leisure" which is a privilege of our affluent society?

4. Did Jesus have "leisure time"? How did He use it?

5. Imagine that you have the assignment to develop a church program designed to assist Christians in the re-creative use of leisure time. What would your proposal include?

13

Have You Heard
the Prophecy According
to *Sports Illustrated*?

"Hear the words of the prophet as found in *Sports Illustrated*" would certainly be a homiletical no-nod for Sunday morning sleepers. Having developed a here-we-go-again attitude toward Isaiah, Daniel, and Amos, perhaps there is value in listening once in a while to the thunderings of our secular seers.

Either symbolically or accidentally, *Sports Illustrated* has honored Muhammad Ali, a minister of the prophet, as sportsman of the year. In the same issue a predictive statement about the future of sports was featured under the title "From Here to 2000." Even though there are some far-out speculations, such as genetic manipulation that will produce nine-foot basketball players with the hands of concert pianists, most of the predictions have the credibility of being rooted in current facts and trends.

At first reading, the prophecy according to *Sports Illustrated* is more entertaining than provocative. After the ideas settle into the mind, however, the implications begin to develop a moral monster with which Christians will have to contend. So hold your seats and hear the words of the prophet as found in *Sports Illustrated*.

All professional sports will resort to betting in order to pay their costs and hold spectator interest. Two current

111

facts bolster this prediction. One is that professional sports cannot keep paying $3.7 million to "Catfish" Hunters without pricing the average spectator out of the market. My Scotch ancestry has already caused me to rebel at the idea of paying six to eight dollars to watch professional sports. I can find sporting options for eight dollars that will involve my whole family as participants.

The other economic fact of life which professional sports is facing is spectator saturation. Game upon game, league upon league, bowl upon bowl gluts your visual and mental capacities after a while. Thousands of fans stayed home from football games last fall when the snow flew or when their teams dropped out of contention. (At last, Sunday football caught up with the church.) Even the Super Bowl has lost its glamour. With machine-like defensive games, artificial excitement has to be stimulated. How charged up did you get when you heard that Dwight White of the Pittsburgh Steelers had a virus or that Fran Tarkenton had a sore arm?

Desperation from zooming costs and waning interest will force professional sports into gambling, according to the predictors. Taking their cue from the racetracks, promoters will count upon pari-mutuel windows, off-field betting, and credit-card betting on home TV to bring multiplied millions of new dollars into their industry. Then, like the racetracks, ticket costs can be sharply reduced to keep the fans coming. "No-shows" at the games will also be reduced, because spectator interest will depend upon winners and point-spreads even among "also-rans" for the championship.

Violence will increase in sports as dehumanization continues. Evel Knievel's "death-leap" over the Snake River had a bit of prophecy in it. Knievel had no fans, but he successfully hustled his haters. For the thousands who attended the debacle, the millions who watched by closed circuit TV, and the collective ear of the nation which waited for the results, Evel was the sole character in a Snake River morality play. It was man defying the inevitability of death, symbolic of both divine and human systems.

As sports become more technical and athletes become more super, brutality will be the surprise to break the monotony. A few years ago, the NFL would not let a player take a violent-sounding nickname. Today, "Mean Joe" Green is a national celebrity. Hockey was once known for the finesse of a Maurice Richard, but now all of the teams are trying to match the brute force of the world champion Philadelphia Flyers with their super-smasher, Dave Schultz, a disowned product of Sunday school and youth camp. Muhammad Ali's selection as Sportsman of the Year for 1974 has already put blood, bashes, and bruises back on the throne of athletics — a prediction of things to come.

As professional sports become more mechanical, commercial, and brutal, people will turn to play again. Two extremes are predicted for the sports of the future. Technosports will be countered by Ecosports. We can envision the extension of Technosports with domed stadiums, air-conditioned climates, instant replays over the scoreboard, artificial turf, computerized dugouts, and wired-up spectators who can hear the quarterback's signals. One visionary even foresaw "feelies" in sports by the twenty-first century, when we will be able to feel the athlete's heartbeat, adrenalin, and pain. What a thrill it would be to feel Ali's punch in the face! Nothing, however, could beat the kick you'd get from the "feelies" if Evel

Knievel were killed.

As Technosports push athletics into a Buck Rogers world, people will react by natural, unstructured play. Ecosports have no preset rules, no scores, and no winners. One hundred people gather in a park, according to *Sports Illustrated,* to play Never-Never games — never played before and never to be played again. Like hippies throwing Frisbees, we will play with the wind — doing what we want to do, whenever we want to do it, and no one will judge the quality of our performance.

Moral questions arising from these sports prophecies challenge our Christian values. Will we move with the tide and accept gambling in professional sports? To date, Christian leadership in the pulpit or in print has said little about the commercialization, saturation, and dehumanization of big-time sports. To the contrary, a professional athlete who is a Christian gains instant honor in our circles. Witnessing Christians are managers, coaches, superstars, and players in the games. Ironically, professional football, the predicted leader in Technosports, probably has more Christians participating and more prayer meetings in locker rooms than any other sport. What will be their response if they earn their livelihood from gambling dollars? More specifically, will Christians go to the arena to watch the gladiators draw blood? Will we have the moral conviction to speak out against the "bread and circuses" mentality of modern Rome?

Technosports may be too big or too distant an issue to concern us. Leisure time is not. Behind all the prophecies is the assumption that Americans will have a time vacuum that will be filled with some kind of activity. By A.D. 2000, the leisure-work ratio may be 2-1 with over 200 days off each year for the average worker. For those of us who grew up with a work-orientation, we feel guilty when we are not working. So, we justify leisure-time activities as necessary in order to do better work. Creative and positive leisure, however, is an end in itself. Human beings need both work and leisure for a balanced life, but both lose their value when we work to play or play to work. Without an understanding of leisure, Americans go from work to inactivity, not from work to leisure. If we are honest, we would confess that we do not know how either to rest or to play. Inactivity makes us easy prey for mass manipulators who know how to create vicarious participation for frustrated spectators while dulling their minds to the moral questions.

I am sure that very few sports promoters are fiendish monsters bent upon the destruction of our national morals. They are businessmen who survive only when they can turn their dollars into profits. From experience, we know that they may not stop to consider the morality of the means until corruption or public opinion pushes them against the wall. Therefore, the preacher who dared to begin his sermon with the call, "Hear the words of the prophet as found in *Sports Illustrated*," would also have to proclaim, "Hear the Word of the Lord." Now, before the sports prophecies are fulfilled, Christian leaders should call a conference on a Christian Ethic for Work and Leisure; pastors should grapple with the moral questions that confront Christians with time on their hands; and, as individual Christians, we should rework our convictions about sports, money, and leisure so that our actions are guided by the time of the Spirit, not the spirit of the times.

QUESTIONS

1. Is it fair to compare our overfed, oversaturated sports society with the "bread and circuses" of decadent Rome? If so, is the next step toward totalitarianism inevitable or are there redeeming features that still exist in our society?

2. Predictions of increased violence in professional sports continue to come true. Is there evidence of public reaction against the brutality or does it expose our enjoyment of smashes, crashes, and bloodletting?

3. Professional, and now intercollegiate sports, are dominating media time on weekends and holidays. What is the impact of this intrusion into church and family life? Do church leaders dare to call for a reversal of the trend in Christian homes? What Biblical principles should guide our decisions about the time and money spent on entertainment, such as sports?

4. Christians have not usually patronized sports, such as horse racing, dominated by gambling. Would you patronize the professional sports of football, basketball, and baseball if their financial basis shifted from the price of a ticket to a bet on the outcome? Why, or why not?

5. Why have professional athletes, particularly football players, become a visible front for Christian witness when commercialism, violence, and Sunday competition seem so contrary to conservative Christianity?

14

Has Even Satanism
Gone to the Devil?

"Satan, 3; God, 1" is the box score in the latest poll of American beliefs. While God barely holds His own, Satan has moved like a streaker in public opinion. Out of nowhere, he has come — visible, exposed, and running. A few months ago, less than 20 percent of our population believed in the devil. Today, the number has doubled and, surprisingly, among the better-educated people of our populace.

If we had been watching, we would have seen the new Satanism coming. *Hair,* the rock opera, predicted the rise of ungodly, supernatural forces in the astrological Age of Aquarius. *Rosemary's Baby* added witchcraft and demon possession to our visual experience. But it took *The Exorcist* to bring the devil back to center stage. Not only do we believe in him again; we have honored him with an Oscar! Satan may be our new folk hero replacing John Wayne. Someday there may be a bumper sticker on a blue Volkswagen which reads, "The Devil or The Duke." Christians might say, "I told you so," when belief in the devil returns to the American mind. But it's not that easy. The devil is too smart to depend upon the fickleness of public opinion for his sense of well-being. He knows that today's hero is tomorrow's goat. He also knows that the silent movements of the serpent are more effective than the ferocious roaring of the lion. If C. S. Lewis were alive, I'm sure that he would have Screwtape pen an urgent wire to his nephew on earth reading, *"Operation*

Exorcist has backfired. Stop. Return to undercover role.''

If the devil isn't responsible for his sudden return to popularity, who is? My opinion is that man is recreating the devil in his own image. This does not mean that Satan is just a perverted father figure — a figment of a Freudian imagination. To me, he is as real as God himself and as personal as Jesus' tempter in the wilderness. But when we trace the biblical profile of Satan, it doesn't match the Hollywood version. Satan is alive and well today because we are using him to explain the mess we're in. I have my own theories of why the devil is having his day.

Green Slime Theory. Because of several warnings from astute friends, I have not seen *The Exorcist.* Like you, however, I am spurred on by the warnings. One of these days, I'll muster the emotional strength to fight the devil in fantasy as well as in reality. Right now, I have my hands full. But when the time comes, I'll put on my false nose, black mustache, and horn-rimmed glasses in order to stand in line *incognito* for the movie. In the meantime, I'll have to be content with magazine reviews. As I understand it, a nauseous climax of the film comes when the demon-possessed girl vomits green slime and masturbates with a crucifix. *Voila, Selah, Ole,* and *Amen!* We have come to the end of the maze in the search of the senses. Green slime is certainly the most bitter vetch of the alcoholic's ''hangover,'' the addict's ''sweats,'' and the sensualist's ''blahs.'' It is the devil's reward when the senses have been shocked beyond tolerable limits. If hell has its own issue of *Variety* magazine, I doubt that *The Exorcist* got a five-star rating. But as an explanation for a sinful journey through the senses, green slime is the dead end where men again recognize the demon who drives them.

Missing Tapes Theory. Watergate is only a symptom of our polluted moral air. Traveling from one Washington to another, I find pessimists in despair and optimists uncertain. No one wants to admit that we may be personally responsible for our dilemma. Like the children of Israel when they showed Moses their golden calf, we have pointed to our own creation and cried, "Look what the fire has done!" A scapegoat is needed to take our sins away and if we can't blame the President, we resurrect the devil. General Alexander Haig spoke for us all when he reasoned that the eighteen and one-half-minute gap in the presidential tape was caused by some "sinister force." Perhaps it was a black devil who specializes in White Houses!

Satan's ego must be inflated by this unearned recognition at the highest level of government. We sin and give him the credit. But does he (or a liberated she?) really want to be just another scapegoat? If the biblical account of his origin is an accurate picture of his personality, Satan wants to be recognized as a sovereign person, not a sinister force. He does not want to be our scapegoat, he wants to be our lord.

Occult Revival Theory. Christians do not have a corner on revivals. Sociologists have labeled the return of Satan as a revival of the occult. While popular belief in a personal devil may be novel for our generation, it is not new in history. Revivals of the occult occurred at the waning of the Roman Empire and the rise of the Renaissance. In each era, a stable society was disrupted by values that were changing faster than traditional institutions could absorb them. Social evolutionists see these disruptions as mutations in the development of the human species. They say that revivals, whether divine or diabolic, are temporary setbacks up the ladder of progress. In the long run, however, man will survive with new symbols, new beliefs, and new values. Satan will have his day, just as God has had His moment of glory, but ultimately, evolutionary forces will be triumphant. According to this theory, today's devil is an evolutionary accident which will eventually become extinct as the dodo bird.

— *Paradise Lost Theory*. Stuff for Utopian dreams comes from the belief that man is good and evil is a flaw in the environment. Currently, Utopian dreams are dead. Wilson envisioned a war to end wars; Roosevelt dreamed of a chicken in every pot; social gospelers foresaw the kingdom of God on earth; secularists had hopes for mankind "come of age"; and student radicals thought that they were tillers of the soil for the "greening of America." Each paradise is now lost. Neither reform nor revolution has ushered in the millennium. Consequently, we are living with disillusionment, the distillation of lost dreams. In these moments, we turn inwardly for a reason. What we see is not pretty. Our hearts are peopled by demons which need to be exorcised. Although few Utopians would identify with Charles Manson, in the mirror of his paranoia, we see the lost hopes of our Utopian dreams. At his pretrial examination, Manson said, "If God is one, what can be bad?" Manson may have been mad, but he called Utopians to judgment by posing the problem of evil which the dreamers denied. When the attempt is made to eliminate evil by social reform, international treaties, or psychological conditioning, Utopian dreams are smashed by crime, war, and rebellion. The alternative is no better. When Manson made God, good, and evil one, the Tate murder was a righteous act.

So Satan, like a perverted phoenix bird, arises out of the ashes of burned-out Utopias. Or, as a journalist who reviewed the Manson case said, "Dreams of heaven often pave the road to hell." On that road, we meet the devil face to face.

Satan in Scripture. Biblical accounts of Satan have some similarities to contemporary theories. Demons may be a part of madness, as they were for the man of Gadara. In his case, the devil occupied the no-man's land between fantasy and reality. Perhaps he was an early victim of green slime.

Sane men, according to the Scriptures, can also be victims of the devil. If Jesus had succumbed to the temptation of Satan, His potential for changing men would have been twisted for evil ends even though His means might have continued under the guise of goodness. When moral confusion reigns among men of power, a "sinister force" may be the substitute for Satan.

Moral neutrality is an open invitation for Satanic control, according to the Word of God. In the parable of the heart purged of a demon, neutrality results. The wandering devil, however, joins in league with seven other demons and brings them home to the empty heart. Consequently, the last state of the man is worse than the first.

Modern man's preoccupation with Satan seems to fit best with the parable of the empty heart. Recently, the spiritual condition of the secularist in our society has been described as desacralized. Presumably, transcendent beings and sacred values have been purged from his existence. Moral neutrality is the result. Values have meaning only in the functional present. Condemned to live with the consequences of his choices, he finds that moral neutrality leads to spiritual bankruptcy. Then the supernatural returns, not to save him as God might have done, but to damn him as devils do. Exorcism is the court of last resort for a self-condemned secularist.

Perhaps, then, the moral of the Satan story is best expressed in the quip which contains a bundle of truth, "Be kind to your exorcist; you can be repossessed."

QUESTIONS

1. Is it coincidental that a revival of evangelical Christianity and occult religions is taking place at the same time? Are they cultural accidents or true-and-false responses to the same human need? If the latter, what is the human need to which both respond?

2. How does Jesus' Parable of the Wandering Devils (Matt. 12:44, 45) who returned with seven cohorts to a vacant heart apply to our contemporary secular society?

3. If you develop a theology of Satan based upon Jesus' encounters with him and His teaching about him, what is Satan's M.O. (mode of operation) against Christians in the world?

4. Jesus never minced words with Satan. What help does His experience give us for dealing with the attacks, the flattery, and the seduction of Satan?

5. Satanism appears to be a degenerate phase of a society that has moved downward from alcohol, drugs, and sex. After Satanism, what?

15

Are the Signs of the Times Written in the Wind?

One of Bob Dylan's songs begins, *"You don't need a weatherman to know which way the wind blows."* This biblical paraphrase inspired the radicals of the New Left to name their guerrilla forces the "Weathermen." With a wet finger in the wind, they declared war on our society with boards, brickbats, and bombs. Even though they are a far cry from the spirit of evangelical Christianity, the Weathermen Movement has taught us a lesson.

Jesus said, "Ye can discern the face of the sky; but can ye not discern the signs of the times? A wicked and adulterous generation seeketh after a sign; and there shall no sign be given unto it, but the sign of the prophet Jonas" (Matthew 16:3-4). Then, with a rare show of impatience, He spun on His heel and left the scene. In effect, Jesus said, "You don't need a weatherman to know which way the wind blows." The signs of the times are obvious. An eye on the sky and a finger in the wind is the alert stance for Christians who are part of *Operation Skywatch*.

You don't need a weatherman to know that evangelicals are no longer exempt from social issues. The gust of wind that came from the United States Congress on Evangelism may have signaled a turning point in the history of evangelical Christianity. Feel the drive for action that exists among Christian youth today and you will know that isolationism is dead. It was just a matter of time anyway. Evangelical Christianity was like the ostriches in the cartoon in the *Saturday Review*. One ostrich had just brought his head out of the sand and had one eye swollen shut. His companion ostrich chided him, "How many times have I told you to keep your eyes shut when you put your head in the sand?" Now, our heads are out and our eyes are open. With sight comes responsibility.

You don't need a weatherman to know the issues that evangelical Christianity must confront. Race is a top priority item on the national agenda. James Foreman's *Black Manifesto* seemed easy to resolve because of the language of revolution and violence. Yet, in education, blacks are asking for reduced standards in admission, retention, and graduation. In employment, they are asking for quotas without regard for qualifications. In business, they are asking for risk capital without strings. In religion, they are asking for the compensation of a black God.

War is as hot an issue as race. The debate over war has split families and friends. Viewpoints can vary from alignment with the doves who demand immediate reductions in defense spending to those who would use atomic weapons at the rattle of a sabre. Christians held every shade of opinion on Vietnam. If they were for withdrawal, they risked association with the ultraleft. If they were for winning, they were in danger of alignment with the radical right.

Revisions in drug laws are moving contrary to the traditional evangelical Christian stance. Some legislators have proposed a distinction between marijuana and hard-line drugs. With an estimated twenty million marijuana users in the nation, the pressure for change has mounted steadily. To this point, the evangelical response to drugs has been rage and condemnation. Should the stance be altered? What are the implications?

At home, sex education and sensitivity training are issues that generate considerable heat. Sex education has been going on in public schools for many years, but suddenly it has become explicit. Sensitivity training is as ancient as self-criticism, but suddenly it has become professional and popular. Again, Christians can be found lining up on all sides of these issues. There are those who read a communist plot in the public school movement. There are those who decry the default of the home. There are others who are equally quick to defend the values of these learning experiences.

That's just the beginning. Abortion, genetic manipulation, energy conservation, cloning, euthanasia, and individual privacy illustrate the items in a bulging, ethical catalog.

You don't need a weatherman to know that evangelical Christianity is entering a new era of testing. In the past, evangelical Christianity was deeply embroiled in controversies with the scientific community over the theory of evolution and with liberal Christianity over the nature of revelation. The controversy now is no longer academic. Evangelical Christianity must test its viability in the streets. This will undoubtedly create new internal strains on the delicate fabric of the movement. The Vietnam moratorium was a warning at this point. I took the position that the Vietnam issue was of national importance and required a serious discussion among Christians. The result was a threat of flags planted on the lawn and a knife at my throat — all in the name of God. The difference between conviction and prejudice became obvious. You can talk about a conviction without getting mad.

Social involvement also means a risk that we have not known. How do you respond to a black man who tells you, "We are in a losing battle, so I would just as soon kill you as look at you'"? How do you recapture your cool when you tell a black man that his son is a "sharp, little boy" and he bristles, "Don't you ever call my son a 'boy' '"? The tests will come from prejudice within and hostility without.

You don't need a weatherman to know that evangelical Christianity needs a theology of social involvement. Our theology of personal integration is strong and viable. We understand the totality of human need and the implications of spiritual recovery. We work constantly to change the tactics of evangelism in order to remain relevant. We do not hesitate to count the results. By comparison, the approach to social involvement is pitifully weak. We have not defined the totality of social needs and the implications for the spiritual climate. We have limited our tactics in social action to a few hit-and-miss techniques on safe issues. We have never dared to evaluate our effectiveness.

It is time for evangelical scholars to review and rewrite a biblical theology for social action. Theoretical scholarship will not be enough. The theory needs to be tested by example. At the same time, evangelical scholars in other disciplines need to present analyses of social issues in layman's language from a biblical point of view. Ignorance and prejudice go hand in hand. It would be most helpful if Christian periodicals published articles on race, war, sex education, sensitivity training, and drugs where the conclusion could not be read in the first paragraph. This kind of writing is necessary for understanding. War has a historical, cultural, and political background that must be understood before a position is taken. Black protest includes an economic dilemma that a white man can hardly understand. Drug laws have medical as well as social factors that enter into decision-making. Sex education relates to the changing role of the family in contemporary society. Without some understanding of these problems, evangelical involvement will be only *sanctified prejudice*.

The crucial point is that evangelical Christianity must become involved in social issues as an *option* rather than a *reaction*. We are accused of being Republican, middle-class, big business, white, and militaristic. If so, our reaction to social issues will be tagged as a form of "knee-jerk conservatism." Evangelical Christianity will come of age when it cannot be labeled left or right. With a wet finger in the wind, it should cut across establishments and antiestablishments as it responds to the signs of the times with a genuine biblical option in truth and in action.

QUESTIONS

1. What do you consider the five most crucial ethical issues facing evangelical Christians today?

2. Moral standards dictated by the institutions of the home, the church, and the school are losing their power just when individuals are being asked to make the most difficult ethical choices in the history of man. How can the home, the church, and the school teach moral development so that individuals can make choices in the new and changing ethical dilemmas which the future will bring?

3. Sorokin, the sociologist, traced the movement of societies from Ideational (ruled by ideals) to Sensate (ruled by the senses), with an Ideational age (mixed rule of ideals and senses) in between. In which stage would you describe our age? Can a spiritual revival restore ideals in a society? Do we have any evidence that the

127

evangelical resurgence in the last quarter of the twentieth century is affecting the moral tone of the society?

4. Evangelical Christians are said to number between 45 and 50 million adult Americans. What are the pros and cons of attempts to rally evangelical institutions as a power block to influence American life through political and economic action? Or is it God's design to disperse His church as He did in the Book of Acts through internal conflict and external persecution in order to spread the gospel?

5. How does a Christian use the resources of the Scriptures and the Holy Spirit for making ethical choices for which there is no previous pattern of experience?

16

Will the Last Person
to Leave
Please Turn Out the Light?

When the SST was squashed by Congress, our city of Seattle sank into economic depression. At the bottom of the trough and at the height of the exodus, a pessimist rented space on a billboard at the entrance to the city and posted the words, "Will the last person to leave please turn out the light?"

Some evangelical Christians would just as soon turn out the light and throw the world into the darkness of its last night. Others, however, have just rediscovered the "on" switch; for instance, the National Association of Evangelicals.

A novelist described a luxurious American embassy in an impoverished land as the only building on the street that could afford to have its lights on at night. "But," he said, "the lights of the embassy were shining in upon itself!"

Evangelical Christianity has been described as a light of hope in a dark land. When it comes to critical social issues, however, the light has shone in upon itself.

This image is changing. There are now some rays of light that are flickering down to the streets below as well as across the world. The National Association of Evangelicals is grappling with social issues beyond bluenosed laws, communism, and Roman Catholic power. Evangelical denominations are setting up task force committees on social action and weighing their responsibilities for the many faces of poverty on the domestic scene. Informal groups of evangelical Christians are forming within churches and across denominational lines to attack specific social ills and to follow with a redemptive witness. Then, there is the growing force of unsung heroes of evangelical Christianity who involve themselves as individuals in social concerns. These persons carry our witness without labels or credits.

Many of these thrusts are still feeble, expedient, and imitative. Evangelical Christian social action is sometimes feeble because the issues run so deeply and extend so far that only massive resources can produce significant change. "Band-Aid" social action does not get at the cancer of the organism. Furthermore, the efforts of evangelicals still tend to be expedient, because there is a convenient selection of the least controversial issues. Money for a ghetto project or discussions with minority groups are accepted as daring forays into social action. But, if discrimination in employment or housing were attacked, the witness would be fragmented beyond recognition. I can still feel the sting of the words that I overheard from two evangelical leaders at a national convention. They were congratulating themselves on the fact that they could listen to the testimony of Senator Mark Hatfield despite his liberal political views.

Evangelical social action attempts also tend to be imitative. The executive of the Model Cities Project in Seattle told me that there were fifty-two programs that had been imported for the Central Area in education alone. He said that concerned groups tend to follow the same pattern, so the inner city is a victim of social "overkill." Now, he is looking for groups that are willing to bring the ghetto to the suburbs with the hope that the attitudes of both ghetto and suburban dwellers can be changed. Otherwise, "going to the ghetto" may actually be a new form of white protectionism. In reviewing our efforts in social action, we are usually among the followers rather than the leaders.

These observations lead to specific suggestions for capitalizing on the awakening social conscience of evangelical Christians.

1. *Evangelical Christians must prepare for social action as diligently as they would prepare for personal evangelism.* When I asked a black man what Christians could do, he answered, "Do your homework." He was talking about the confessions of bias, the elimination of discrimination in the local church, and the understanding of the black culture. "Do your homework" can be extended to all areas of Christian social action. We must know our motives. If Christian action is an emotional jag or a popular fad, our motives will never stand the grinding rub of hostility and frustration that involvement requires. This means that Christian social action begins at home. Racial discrimination in the local church vetoes any effort to end discrimination in the ghetto. One pastor told me that his Sunday school bus picked up children five miles south, but only five blocks north of the church. The northern limit was the Negro neighborhood! For that church, sermons on the equality of men in Christ, missionary conventions, or action on other social issues are hollow mockeries to the black man looking at the church over the barricade of five city blocks.

Those who would act must be thoroughly acquainted with the problems they seek to solve. Anyone who intends to work with blacks, for instance, should read everything from Eldridge Cleaver's *Soul On Ice* to William Pannell's *My Friend, the Enemy*. As Richard Leakey, the African explorer, said about the role of the white in Kenya, ". . . if he has to have a white face, he must have a black mind." Because social action for Christians is always in an alien arena with a hostile cheering section, an effective witness must be acquainted with that arena and the rules of the game.

Weak souls and wavering spirits will never survive this basic training for Christian social action. But, for the strong souls who are still ready to take the risk, the final step in preparation is to build a biblical perspective for social action. Obviously, each previous step must be interlaced with insight and leading through the Word of God. In addition, the Christian must have the support of a biblical perspective so that the redemptive focus is kept in view and the work is always seen within the total task of the church in the world. Evangelical Christians are guilty of avoiding the Word of God both when seeking out their social responsibility and when trying to fulfill it. Perhaps change begins by dropping the loaded phrase "social action" and becoming serious about the Christian's "biblical concerns."

2. *Evangelical Christians must relate social action to the integral life of the church.* In most cases, Christian social action on hot, domestic issues began as an *ad hoc* or unsanctioned effort of a few people outside of the church. But Christian social action works two ways. It must save men inside as well as outside the church. To do this, the activities of the church need to be revised. As it is now, almost 100 percent of the church activities are aimed toward organizational self-perpetuation. Even a social action committee can guarantee immunity from involve-

ment through perpetual talk; or an ad hoc social action unit can maintain protectionism by giving the church a built-in "guilt-absorber."

A start on total church involvement in social action would be to reduce the obligations of members for church activities to one responsibility per member. In its place, the church would ask the member to serve as a volunteer in some crucial area of community life. Voluntary social service is a unique feature of American democracy, but there are never enough volunteers to meet the need. As I've watched social matrons, gray ladies, and candy-stripers at work in such programs as mental health clinics, hospital wards, retarded children's camps, and in family service agencies, I've often said, "What a difference it would make if redeemed people brought their love into this area of human need." Until you share the struggle of a crippled child, bear the bitterness of a deserted wife, hear the threat of a black man to kill you, or feel the lostness of a hopeless addict, Christian social action is an academic question. Thus, if churches would legitimize and sanctify the Christian in voluntary social service, the effect might be more revolutionary than pushing doorbells.

3. *Evangelical Christians should focus their social concern on a point of unmet human need in their communities which can lead to redemptive action.* Someone once said, "If you want to get rich, go into a profession that is known for its unethical behavior — and be honest." The adage carries over into Christian social action. The church should not duplicate the agencies that are funded from public sources. Rather, it should seek to influence the direction of these agencies. The point of influence may be the reminder that human need takes

precedence over bureaucracy and that the motive for social service rises highest from a Christian view of man. Or the point of influence may be that of providing professional Christian leadership and voluntary services for the agency.

Despite the massive sweep of the welfare state, many human hurts are still unhealed. Pastors report the growing numbers of alienated people who seek their counsel. Divorce, for instance, is now as easy as "irreconcilable differences" under new laws. Yet, behind the legal term "irreconcilable," there is the alienation, guilt, and suffering that court action cannot heal. The generation gap between parents and children is another kind of "irreconcilable difference" that is one of the most difficult symptoms of a revolutionary age. The new mobility of our society creates a loneliness among migrants who need roots in a new community. These examples point to the endless prospects for evangelical social action today. Individual Christians and individual churches have no excuse for not responding to the special needs of their communities. A Task Force on Human Hurts would quickly discover more work than any one church could accomplish.

Ultimately, Christian social action will be tested by whether or not a climate is created that is conducive to redemption. At one extreme, Christians can fall into the trap of assuming that social action is an end in itself. There is some truth in this, because Christ gave intrinsic value to unevangelistic aid for the hungry, the naked, and the thirsty. Christian love responds first to men as men and to men in need. At the other extreme, Christian social action can be judged by the head count of new converts. A program of biblical concern cannot be just a technique for soul winning — it must be a style of life that reflects the self-sacrificing love of the Christian in action. Between the extremes is the position that biblical social concern develops a climate conducive for redemption. For the individual Christian, it will provide the natural opportunity to explain his motive. For the Church, it will provide a more responsive atmosphere for the proclamation of the good news. Thus, a test for individual and collective Christian social action is to ask, "Will this action improve the climate for redemption?" For instance, if a revision of the welfare system and a plan for a guaranteed annual income meets human need, maintains individual dignity, and breaks down a barrier against the Christian witness, perhaps the church should support it. Or, if the move of blacks against the segregated, skilled trades unions will open the door to economic participation in the community and raise the next question about the poverty of man's spirit, perhaps Christians should run the risk of supporting the move while condemning the violence.

Thoughts like these are probably beyond the present scope of evangelical Christianity. From the far reaches of taking positions on controversial issues, we need first to return to our homework. The hopeful signs of an awakened social conscience among evangelical Christians need to be encouraged wherever they exist. With that encouragement, there needs to be the admonition that evangelical social action must be Christlike in motive, biblical in perspective, and redemptive in outcome.

QUESTIONS
1. Secular columnists have suggested that the balance of religious power has swung to evangelicals. If so, what strategy of leadership would you propose for evangelicals to assume the spiritual and social responsibility that goes with popularity and power?

2. Is there a Biblical basis for giving individual salvation the first priority in the mission of the church with the assumption that social renewal will follow as a natural consequence of redeemed men and women? Does history support such a position?

3. Do you have a social action committee in your church? Have they limited their work to occasional forays against gambling, drugs, pornography, and alcohol? What if they chose to study and take a stand on more controversial issues, such as racial discrimination, women's rights, environmental pollution, land use, and tax reform?

4. Some Christians from Marxist countries have tried to reconcile their faith with the social philosophy of their government. They are quick to note that American Christians have done the same thing with democracy and capitalism. Does the kind of government make any difference to a Christian? Can Christianity be reconciled with Marxism or capitalism?

5. If you were to organize a task force on human hurts in your neighborhood or community, what are some of the unmet needs to which you would minister?

17

Do I Have
to Stay Awake, Lord?

A troubled soul went to a psychiatrist for help. "What's your problem?" the doctor queried. "Well, you see, I don't have the will power to resist temptation, and my conscience is uneasy." Smelling a quick recovery, the psychiatrist diagnosed, "Then you would like to strengthen your will power? Is that right?" His patient paused, dropped his head, and then answered, sheepishly, "Well, not exactly, Doc. If it's all right with you, I'd prefer to have my conscience weakened."

An unawakened conscience is not an option for a Christian. Social responsibility is a biblical imperative that is mandated by the Word, modeled by the Christ, and motivated by the Spirit. Yet, to mention the subject in Christian company is to guarantee debate and controversy, even alienation. The ideal is accepted as an imperative, but the issues are treated as options.

The parable of the Good Samaritan is used as a positive example of Christian social responsibility. It has all of the ingredients of the modern situation — religious snobbery, cultural discrimination, circumstantial disadvantage, and the impact of involvement at a risk. A neglected element in the story, however, is the meaning of the words which describe the response of the priest and the Pharisee as they encountered the mugged man in the middle of the road. "He passed by on the other side" (Luke 10:31) tells us that the priest and the Pharisee had to *go out of their way to miss human need!* The typical picture of a man in the gutter on the side of the road would have given them an excuse for neglecting him. But no, the victim was in the middle of the road and probably they had to go through the gutter to miss him.

How did the priest and the Pharisee rationalize their action as they continued on their journey? Having been in that position myself, I know the steps. First, they felt guilty and said, ''Maybe I should have stopped.'' But guilt is painful, so the second step is a mental gymnastic to find some kind of defense for their behavior. Because they were respected and religious men, their guilt had to be resolved by some kind of theological or moral rationalization. Then, having convinced themselves of the rightness of their action, they put the experience out of their mind and went down to their houses justified by their own mental processes. Without a doubt, the priest and the Pharisee will be among those people at the Judgment who plead with honest surprise, ''Lord, Lord, when didn't we do these things?''

This is the day when certain ideas in economics and management have been translated into the popular concepts. Parkinson's Law, for example, states: ''Work expands to fill the time available to do it.'' More recently, Peter's Principle has been used to describe the problems of a man in the organizational system. Peter's Principle is: ''In a hierarchy, every man rises to his level of incompetence.'' In the same spirit, I would like to propose an addition to the collection based upon the Good Samaritan story. Just in case it catches on, let's call it ''McKenna's Maxim'' because I am one of the worst offenders. The maxim is: *"Christians must go out of their way to miss human need and find religious reasons to justify themselves."*

Assuming that the maxim is accepted as a guide for avoiding Christian social responsibility, some practical advice is needed to develop a sophisticated set of justification techniques. At the risk of being accused of humility, let's call them "David's Dodges" because I am already skilled in their use.

The Theological Sidestep. "The man in the middle of the road is a sinner." Sin is at the root of all of our social problems, and to minister to human need without the opportunity to preach the gospel might be interpreted as theological liberalism by other Christians.

The Spatial Slip. "There's room to get by on the other side." Social problems in certain places become so serious and human need becomes so desperate that the climate is not conducive to the gospel. As long as the frontier was open, one could move away from his social responsibility. When the frontier closed and the masses began coagulating in the city, the suburbs were still open. Now that the suburbs are degenerating, the *spatial slip* may have to give way to the *mental move* until there's room on the moon.

The Economical Evasion. "I gave at the church." The resources of the church are very limited and the priorities have already been established for Christian outreach. If I responded to every need, I would have to reduce my contributions to missions or evangelism and deny some other needy soul.

The Ideological Escape. "He wouldn't accept my help because we are not in the same social class." Like it or not, Christianity is class conscious. Someone at his own level can get through to him better than I can. Maybe when I get home, I'll call the mission.

The Chronological Circumvention. "If I help him now,

I'll lose my effectiveness with other people." Social timing plays an important part in Christain action, and as soon as someone else leads the way, you can count on me to help.

The Substitutionary Swerve. "I am already carrying my social responsibility." Christians must budget their time, money, and energy in order to be good stewards. As a member of the Board, a cheerful giver, and an untiring worker, there is a limit.

The Literary Lam. "When I get home, I'm hoping to write a letter protesting the crime wave." Christians are people who believe in the power of words as well as in the power of the *Word*. Letters to editors, articles for the denominational news, telegrams to congressmen, or a column in a national evangelical magazine are the most effective instruments for Christian concern. After all, a poignant pen reaches more people than a helping hand.

Justification by "David's Dodges" is guaranteed to be an adequate defense against Christian social responsibility. Therefore, only one problem remains before total exemption from social responsibility is available to every Christian. What "dodge" can be developed for the question, "Lord, when didn't we do these things?"

QUESTIONS

1. What is the prophetic role of the church today in warning people of our age of the judgment to come?

2. During the days of campus protest, a student said, "Don't forget, our anger may be just a cry for help." What are some of the unusual ways in which people around us are crying for help?

3. In the final judgment scene in Matthew 25, neither the righteous nor the sinners recalled meeting the needs of the naked, sick, hungry, and imprisoned. Does it mean that there is a naturalness of Christian response to human need that cannot be planned, taught,

or practiced? Or does it mean that we develop habits of compassion or indifference toward people for which we expect neither reward nor punishment?

4. Have you ever thought, if Christians tithed their waking time, more than eleven hours per week would be available for special ministries of Christian witness. Assume that a "Tithe of Time" was given by the members of your church congregation, what priorities would you give to the ministries of the church? What new ministries would you introduce? What new talents would become available to the church? How would your church increase its witness and impact in your community?

5. WHY NOT DO IT?